D1491871

Tenders of the Flock

TENDERS of
the FLOCK

BY LEO J. TRESE

SHEED AND WARD · LONDON · 1957

FIRST PUBLISHED 1956
BY SHEED AND WARD LTD.,
33 MAIDEN LANE,
LONDON, W.C.2
REPRINTED 1957

NIHIL OBSTAT
 Leo J. Ward
 Censor Librorum

IMPRIMATUR
 ✠Alexander M. Zaleski
 Vicar General of Detroit

December 7, 1954

PRINTED IN GREAT BRITAIN BY
LOWE AND BRYDONE (PRINTERS) LIMITED, LONDON, N.W.10

CONTENTS

	page
First Things First	*1*
The Happy Priest	*10*
The Prayerful Priest	*21*
The Persevering Priest	*32*
The Sacrificing Priest	*44*
The Dissatisfied Priest	*56*
The Resolute Priest	*68*
The Generous Priest	*78*
The Repentant Priest	*89*
The Prudent Priest	*101*
The Brotherly Priest	*112*
The Unsecular Priest	*124*
The Catholic Priest	*135*
The Alert Priest	*146*
The Perspiring Priest	*157*
The Marian Priest	*169*
The Ardent Priest	*180*

ACKNOWLEDGMENTS

The contents of this book first appeared in article form in *Emmanuel*, official monthly of the Priests' Eucharistic League.

Tenders of the Flock

FIRST THINGS FIRST

THE ONLY PRIEST I know really well is myself; so I should be careful about making general statements. But because I feel that I am pretty much an average priest, I think it is safe for me to say that very few of us give God the best that is in us; very few of us operate at top capacity. I don't mean that we don't keep busy; most of us live a very full and a very active day. But I do think that if an efficiency engineer, such as industrialists employ, were to make a time-study of us, on any given day, he could show us how to double our effectiveness.

Of course, he would have to be a very special kind of efficiency engineer. He would have to deal in such imponderables as grace, and prayer, and the choosing of the better over the good.

But just suppose that we ourselves, without any outside help, were to increase our priestly productivity by twenty-five per cent. Think what that would mean to souls! It would mean the equivalent of ten thousand new priests, suddenly added to the personnel of our American dioceses.

Now I don't believe in underselling ourselves. Humility does not consist in denying the obvious; and it

B

1

seems fairly obvious that today's priest, on the whole, is a pretty sound article. Especially so, when you consider how seductive is the voice of the modern world, as it woos all who will lend an ear.

No, I do not mean that we are tepid, with the nauseating lukewarmness so roundly cursed by the Holy Spirit in the Apocalypse. I would not even say that we are mediocre, if by mediocrity is meant the halfway point between where we started and where we ought to be. Because I think that we are much closer than halfway to the top. In fact, that is where the real tragedy lies: that we should come so close to the summit, and then rest content; like an Alpine climber who would laboriously toil upwards for fifteen thousand feet, and then abandon the ascent when only five hundred feet from the peak.

Or maybe I shouldn't say that we rest content. I don't suppose that any priest ever says to himself, "I'm good enough now; this is as far as I go." And I am sure that none of us consciously bargain with God the way a good union man might bargain with his employer: "You've had the eight hours work you paid for; now the rest of my time belongs to me." Even in the secrecy of our own hearts, we should never dream of saying to God, "I've already given You all that You have any right to expect; I've got to save a little of myself for me."

No, our trouble isn't so much a matter of compromising with God as it is temporizing. We aren't, actually, satisfied with ourselves. We know that we could do better, and be better. We do not deny that we should take those last few rugged steps, make that last sharp climb that will mean a complete surrender of ourselves to God. We do not exclude the intention of doing so, either. In at least a vague sort of way we do envision the day when we shall rid ourselves of our petty self-attachments and become the priest we know we could be. But always the day is in the indefinite future—very indefinite, and very much future.

Meanwhile we plod along in our priestly duties, planning and executing with a fair degree of conscientiousness, but with nothing like the joy and exhilaration that should characterize our lives. Like the mountain climber who has stopped short of the summit, we suffer the hardships without the taste of triumph. In witness of that fact, we have only to look around us. How many priests do we not know, who are hard-working and duty-minded, and yet seem to find their work a drudgery and their duty a burden? And how many priests do we know who plainly and consistently radiate a quiet happiness which is not easily disturbed?

By happiness I do not mean the clowning, irresponsible good-nature which we sometimes encounter—and which, incidentally, can have great unhappiness at its root. I mean rather the kind of man whose basic happiness shows itself in a mixture of confidence and contentment which does not need frequent vacations and periodic "a few days off" for its renewal. I do not think that there are many priests who are downright unhappy. But I do think that there are many heavy-spirited priests; I do think that too many of us, too often, are moody and depressed—too often with an urge to "get away from it all." For proof, we may have to look no farther than ourselves.

And yet, ours is the vocation whose potential for happiness (and I mean happiness in this life) is practically unlimited. Even on the natural level, there is no other vocation that can give so much of the deep satisfaction that accompanies a work that is truly significant and important; no other vocation that can offer such outlet to a man's highest urges. And on the supernatural level there is the worry-free lightness of spirit which always accompanies the doing of God's work in God's way.

If we have to admit to ourselves that our days are not joyous days, or at least days of quiet contentment; if we have to admit that we find our priesthood, more often than we should, a burden; then it would seem that a little stock-taking is in order. I shouldn't be surprised if the result of such a self-examination might lead us to the conclusion that we have been living too much by faith, and not enough by love.

We have faith, unquestionably. Without faith, we never would have become priests. Without faith, we would not now be active in the priesthood. But, for a fruitful and a happy ministry, faith is not enough. It is basic, it is essential, but it is not enough. Unless my faith is informed by an ardent love, I am much like a man suffering from anemia, going through his day without vibrancy and without savor.

When I talk about love, of course, I am talking about love for God, love for God especially in the Person of Jesus Christ, love for Christ that is a profoundly personal love. It is this love that will make our days joyful, as we go about doing the work of Him Whom we love, seeing things through His eyes, having no interests but His at heart.

Without this love, there will be far too much of human wisdom in our work. When we are cheerful, our cheerfulness will be too much like the professional cheerfulness of the physician or the dentist. When we are cautious, our caution will be too much like the professional caution of the lawyer. When we are zealous and full of plans, our zeal will be too much like the feverish activity of the business man, intent on extending his business. I do not mean that there are not Christian and dedicated doctors and lawyers and business men. I only mean that the purely worldly wisdom which too often characterizes the work of those engaged in secular pursuits, has no place in the work of a priest.

See what happens when we try to live by faith alone, and implement that faith with human wisdom instead of love: First of all we lose our sense of proportion, our ability to distinguish between what is essential and what is only important or desirable. Our Mass, for example, becomes just another duty of our day. We shall offer our Mass with becoming decency and with conscientious regularity, so as not to disappoint our parishioners. But we feel no sense of loss if we miss offering Mass while on vacation; we do not advert to the fact that souls may be robbed of grace, may even be lost, because of the Mass we've skipped. Since we have come to regard our Mass as a duty of our pastoral office, its omission on vacation becomes as logical as the omission of any other duty.

Our Divine Office, too, becomes a drudgery, if our faith is uninspired by love. Since its recitation binds under pain of sin, we shall not easily miss saying our Office. But because we feel that "we get nothing out of it," we can grow very careless in the way in which we pray our breviary. In the coldness of our faith, we forget that the essence of liturgical prayer is not that we should "get something out of it"; the purpose of liturgical prayer is to give glory to God. We need to be more mindful of the significance of that phrase of the *Gloria* of the Mass: "*Gratias agimus tibi, propter magnam gloriam tuam!*" We give thanks to God, not primarily for what He has done for us, but rather we thank Him for His infinite glory. That indeed is our highest vocation and our final destiny—to glorify God. If our eyes, made keen by love, have clearly seen the truth of this, then we shall not look for personal fruit and private delectation from our breviary. Unhurriedly, apart from distracting interruptions, with reverent disposition of body as well as mind, we shall recite our Office, quite content if it does no more than give praise to God. What more could we ask?

I have mentioned our Mass and our Office merely as two obvious examples of how *routine* our days can be, unless love is the motif, the background brightness of all our hours. The seeds of that love, that lively personal love for Christ, are within us, of course. But it is only in unremitting prayer that the love will be nurtured and will grow. The truth of the matter is that we don't, most of us, pray enough. (And please remember that I am including myself in all that I say.) We do not spend enough time in personal prayer.

We pay lip-service to prayer. We acknowledge, in theory, the value of mental prayer, in which we absorb the mind and spirit of Christ, and of spiritual reading —which provides the refurbishment of thought upon which fruitful mental prayer depends. We acknowledge, too, and perhaps sometimes preach upon, the graces and inspirations to be gained from visits to Jesus in the Blessed Sacrament.

But let me ask myself a pointed question. Looking back over the past thirty days, can I say that on at least twenty-eight of those days I have spent a full half-hour (or even twenty minutes) in systematic meditation? During that thirty days, have I read one book that could be honestly classified as spiritual reading? Aside from the time I have spent in preparation for Mass, and thanksgiving afterwards, have I made a daily visit of ten minutes or more to Jesus in the Blessed Sacrament? Have I done it twenty days out of the thirty—two days out of three? Have I even, during the past four weeks, managed to get in the weekly Holy Hour to which I am pledged, as a member of the Priests' Eucharistic League?

If I have to answer no to any of those questions, it will help to pin myself down if I make a rough total of the time I've spent reading secular magazines, the daily paper, listening to the radio or looking at television.

But maybe I haven't wasted time on any of these things. Maybe I've glanced over the newspaper headlines while eating breakfast, and listened to a news broadcast just before going to bed. But every other blessed minute of almost every day, I have been busy, busy, busy. Am I to be blamed, then, if I haven't done as much praying as a monk in a monastery? After all, I've got to take care of my people; these things that I do have got to be done. It's all very well to talk about prayer, but charity comes first. And we don't want to become like these "sacristy priests" we've heard about, who lose touch with their people by keeping their own heads in the clouds.

Others may be more realistic than myself. Others may not have confused themselves with such sophisms as these—sophisms which the merest beginner in logic could untangle with ease.

"Sacristy priest," indeed! As though the Curé of Ars did less for his people, by the long hours he spent in prayer, than I do with all my scurrying hither and yon! The so-called sacristy priests of whom we have heard, who lost contact with their people, did not do so because they spent too much time in prayer. They lost contact because they themselves were of the bourgeoisie, and class-consciousness interposed a barrier between themselves and their people. They painted pictures or raised bees or studied astronomy—and kept the proletariate parishioners in their place.

A European priest who has spent some time in this country told me recently of a marked contrast which he has noted between American and European priests. In this country, the visitor said, he has never seen any learned periodicals or books on rectory reading tables; nothing but popular magazines and practical pastoral journals. In Europe, on the contrary, almost every priest subscribes to one or more scientific reviews, and does a great deal of serious reading and study.

Well, the implied (but friendly) criticism didn't make me feel apologetic. We could do with some more scholarship, we American priests. But scholarship alone will not save souls, any more than sweat alone will do it.

The point is that when we try to excuse our meager prayer-life by pointing to our busy day, and saying that charity comes first, we simply are talking in circles. There is no greater charity we could do our parishioners than to pray for them more. If we spent more time in prayer, a good bit of the work we are doing wouldn't have to be done. Probably a good many of our activities, if examined in the light of prayer, would be recognized as time-wasters and jettisoned entirely. Other activities, planned under the guidance of prayer, would be much more effective and much more successful.

The trouble is that, when we don't pray, there is too much of ourselves in our work, and not enough of God. We undertake some project, and we are determined that it shall be a visible success, no matter how much energy we may have to pour into it. And too often we are satisfied with mere noise and numbers, with little thought of inner fruit. Two hundred men at a Holy Name breakfast is a fine thing. But who will say whether the soul of one fallen-away parishioner, won by an hour of prayer, might not weigh more in the balance?

Perhaps it is this thing of trying to do it all ourselves, and not moving over to make room for God, which accounts also for the time we lose doing things which a layman could do as well—or maybe better. Because it is *our* project, and we are determined that it *must* succeed, we will not risk its execution to laymen. Actually there is so much that we do (at the cost of prayer time) that our laity, plus God, could accomplish much more effectively.

These are the things I keep telling myself, as I try to wiggle and squirm out of the obvious fact that I am not the priest I could be, that I do not pray enough, that I live and work too much by cold faith and not enough by a warming and an enlightening love.

And however slyly I may try to evade the conclusion—in the end I am forced to admit that there is not an hour that I spend on my knees (or on the seat of my pants if I can pray better that way)—there is not an hour I spend in prayer that will not, in the end, spell profit to my people, and happiness to me.

THE HAPPY PRIEST

EVERYONE WANTS to be happy. The desire for happiness is the one universal urge and craving of every human heart. The desire for happiness is at the bottom of every crime, as it is at the bottom of every good action. The bandit, the burglar, the embezzler and the murderer—each of them is looking for happiness as truly as is the virtuous layman or laywoman, the religious novice or the seminarian. The sinner, of course, makes the fatal mistake of seeking happiness through ministration to his self-love, and never does find the happiness he is looking for. The nascent saint seeks happiness through the exercise of his love for God, and *finds* happiness—in direct proportion to the undeviating singleness of his purpose.

It seems ridiculously trite to observe that we priests are human beings. We were human beings before we were priests, and we still retain our human nature after ordination. In us also, then, there is that irresistible pressure towards happiness. If we find happiness it must be, admittedly, within the framework of our priesthood. But I think that we sometimes tend to forget that our happiness, and the basic means of achieving that happiness, are the same for us as for the layman. There are not different kinds of happiness: one kind for the layman, another kind for the religious, and still another kind for the priest.

Nor are there different kinds of "spirituality," if by spirituality we mean the essential means of achieving true happiness. There will be an *accidental* difference in what we might call our short-range objectives, accordingly as a person is a layman, a cloistered nun, or a diocesan priest. There will not be any difference in the tools we use; just a difference in the way we use them.

Even the distinction between the contemplative life and the active life, hallowed though it is by long usage, has often been distorted and misunderstood. Probably no two people in all the world have been so often and so grossly misinterpreted as have poor Martha and Mary. When Christ said that "We ought always to pray," He manifestly was not issuing a universal call to the cenobitic or the monastic life. There must be an element of prayer, of contemplation, in every action that is a truly Christian action; just as there must be a never-satisfied zeal for souls in the life of the most secluded contemplative.

It is a point worth emphasizing—the point that we are first of all Christians, and only secondly are we priests. If we realize that, then we must realize also that to be a good priest, a happy priest, we begin by being a good Christian. The reason for mentioning this rather obvious fact at all, is to guard against two possible errors in judgment in appraising our approach to holiness and happiness. One mistake would be to suppose that there are special mechanics of methods and spiritual exercises attached to growth in sanctity in the priesthood.

If a man supposes that, and then finds himself failing in his efforts to observe an unrealistic rule of life, he may easily grow discouraged and abandon the effort altogether. The other possible error is even more dangerous in its potential results: to suppose that there is something *ex opere operato* about being a priest; as though just being a priest and doing the work of a priest will of itself guarantee that we are *good* priests, holy priests, happy priests.

Would it be too laughably elementary, I wonder, to review our destiny and our duty just as *men*, aside from being priests? To do so we only have to turn to the first page of the little catechism, not to St. Thomas or St. John of the Cross. "Why did God make me?", the little catechism asks. "To know, love and serve God in this world," comes the answer, "in order to be happy with Him in the next."

The key word there, of course, is the word "Love." To *know* God is simply the prelude to loving Him; we cannot possibly love someone we do not know. To *serve* God is the result of loving Him; to do the things that will please the one we love is a necessary corollary to love. And to be happy with God in Heaven is the consequence of love; eternal union with God is the final fruit and issue of our love for God here and now.

God made me, then, to love Him; that is the whole purpose and reason for my existence. It seems obvious that any creature, animate or inanimate, will be at its best doing the things it was made for. A good hunting-dog will make a poor watch-dog; a race-horse pulling a plow would drive a farmer crazy; a razor is a poor tool for peeling potatoes. We can't truthfully speak of happiness, of course, with regard to creatures less than man. However, speaking figuratively, we might say that a hunting-dog will be happiest while hunting; a race-horse will be happiest while racing; a razor will be happiest while cutting whiskers. They will be happiest, in other words, in proportion as they fulfill their nature, in proportion as they do the things they were designed to do.

Rising now from razors and horses and dogs to man, we can say the same thing, and this time in a literal sense: man will be happy in proportion as he fulfills his nature, in proportion as he does the thing he was designed for: which is, to love God. That means to love God with a love that is supremely appreciative, a love that values God above everyone and everything else. It means that all lesser loves, such as love for family or friends, are subordinated to this highest love. Or rather, all lesser loves are incorporated in this greater love and are transformed by it. Our human loves—love for family and love for friends—are directed towards God, very much as the clothes which a man is wearing necessarily move in the direction in which the man is walking. Or perhaps it would be a better example to say that all lesser loves, in relation to our love for God, are like the parts of an automobile in relation to the complete vehicle—each part subordinated to the functioning of the whole car, working together to move the car forward in whatever direction the driver may turn the wheel.

We know (but it will bear repeating) that love for God resides in the will and not in the emotions. How we *feel* towards God is no accurate test of how we *are* towards God. Love for God can and often does overflow from the will into the emotions. The rapturous phrases with which many of the saints have talked about

God indicate how love for God can take possession of
the emotions as well as of the will. But we should make
a great mistake if we thought that we did not love God
simply because our heart did not go pit-pat-pit-pat at
the mention of His Name.

It is not an upsurge of emotion at the thought of God,
but a resolute identification of our human will with the
Will of God, that proves our love for Him. It is the
persevering effort to make God and His Will the very
heart and center of our lives; it is the determined desire
to seek His Will and only His Will regardless of the
cost to ourselves; it is the ability to say, "Dear God, I
want whatever You want, and nothing else"—to be able
to say it and *mean* it: this is the measure of our love for
God. Having thus centered our life in God, our life
will be a harmonious whole; we shall be inwardly at
peace; we shall be happy.

I do not mean that our life will be free necessarily
from all worry, disappointments, unpleasantnesses—much
less free from all physical suffering. That would be
too easy; there would be a universal stampede to love
God if such visible ills of human nature were immediately wiped away. No, love for God will not make us
disembodied spirits, serenely untouched and unmoved by
the fluctuations of life around us. It is not the obstacles
and contradictions and pains of life that make for unhappiness. Freedom from such disturbing factors might
give us an animal contentment—but it would not give
us happiness. Only the unifying, fortifying, illuminating
love of God can do that.

That God's love is a unifying force scarcely seems to
need noting. If God's Will is our goal, and if all our
desires and activities and secondary aims are directed

towards that goal, then ours is a completely integrated and concordant life. That God's love is a fortifying power seems equally evident. We only fear and cringe from that which we do not understand, or from that which threatens our well-being. In the life of him who loves God and seeks His Will only, everything fits, everything has a place; and there is only one fear, the holy fear of what may destroy that love—the fear of treason, of sin. That God's love, again, is an illuminating directive is a truth each of us has personally experienced as we have, in moments of decision, honestly faced the question, "What would God want me to do?"

All right. We were made to give glory to God by giving our love to God. In loving God we fulfill our nature; in loving God we find the highest, the only genuine and lasting happiness. What follows, then? It seems very plain and very simple. But is there any difficulty involved?

To answer that—and if the abrupt transition will not be too jarring—we might turn to the field of clinical psychology for some pointers here. Of course clinical psychologists have their own terminology. To them a person is not a *happy* person; he is a "well-adjusted" person. They do not talk of an *unhappy* person; they will refer to a "maladjusted" person—and if the maladjustment is serious enough, the person will be classified as "emotionally disturbed." The maladjustment is always the result of some unrecognized and consequently unresolved inner conflict. Many such conflicts have no moral connotation and need not concern us here. The only reason for dragging in the psychologists at all is that many people (and we priests are not always exceptions) will take the theories of science more seriously than they will take the principles of religion; the findings of psychology often will carry more weight than the truths of ascetic theology. But in this instance we must in justice admit that the psychologists have done a genuine service in tracing some of the roots of human unhappiness.

An unhappy man (and therefore an unhappy priest) is a man whose inner peace is being disturbed, perhaps destroyed, by a conflict of some kind. It may be a conflict between something he has and something he wants. It may be a conflict between what he is and what he wants to be. It may be a conflict between what he ought to do and what he wants to do. In any case, there can be no peace and therefore no happiness until the conflict is resolved.

We can take it for granted, surely, that each of us has some degree of love for God. We never would have become priests in the first place, and much less would we be priests now, if there were not some motive stronger than self impelling us. But are we as happy in our priesthood as we ought to be, as we could be? If not, then our surrender to God has not been complete. Our embracing of His Will has not been absolute and unconditional. Like particles of dirt floating around in a vial of golden oil, there is still a good bit of self suspended in our love for God, and in need of precipitation.

In other words there is a conflict in our life, a conflict between self and God. What particular form that conflict may take will vary with each of us. It might be profitable for us to consider very briefly one not uncommon way in which self-attachment may war with our attachment to God.

That is the conflict that arises between human loves and divine love. In speaking of human love, I am not referring to what is commonly classified as sensual love, the kind of emotional involvement which in a priest would be outright sin. I am not here dealing specifically with sin. A sinner has to a certain degree resolved his inner conflict—he has resolved it in favor of himself. The habitual sinner, the man who has committed himself to the acceptance and enjoyment of sin, has established a certain degree of peace within himself. Because it is an *unnatural* sort of peace, he cannot know genuine happiness, the happiness that results from the fulfillment of his nature. But there is a sense in which the confirmed sinner is happier than the neophyte saint, who is still engaged in the arduous task of purifying his love for God.

We all are familiar with the conventional hill-billy cartoon which shows "Paw" stretched out in the shade of his ramshackle cabin, a jug of cawn likker beside him, and a lean-ribbed hawg rooting in the arid dust nearby. Against that we can put the picture of the industrious farmer driving his tractor across his broad and well-kept acres; sustained, as he sweats under the hot sun, by the thought of the harvest ahead. The two pictures would offer a good illustration of the peace of the sinner, as against the dissatisfaction of the struggling pilgrim soul.

To go back, then, to the possible conflicts between human love and divine love: I think that it would be a rare thing that a priest's love for his own family would create any barrier between himself and God. There have been unfortunate periods in the history of the Church when nepotism was rampant, and we do occasionally encounter a young priest who seems too much tied to his mother's apron strings. But generally speaking a priest's love for his family is a help rather than a hindrance in his spiritual development. Almost always it is a good Catholic family that has nurtured the priest's vocation to begin with. Some of our greatest strides forward, I think many of us will admit, have been hastened by our efforts to measure up to the high ideals which our family have held up to us. Indeed, a priest who deliberately neglects his own family, and who begins to seek his comfort and relaxation in other homes and other families, is involving himself in the very sort of conflict which we are discussing.

It happens fairly often. There is a family in the parish (or maybe in some other parish) who are friendly, outgoing people. They insist on having Father over some evening and make a big fuss over him, make him feel welcome in their happy family circle. Father feels an answering affection within himself that responds to the affection that is shown him. The next time he has a free evening he drops in again; before very long he is a regular visitor. He may even develop two or three such refuges. And if someone calls at the rectory in urgent need of him, the housekeeper will say, "Father didn't mention where he was going, but you'll probably find him at So-and-so's or at So-and-so's."

Now I am not going to discuss all the evils that can stem from Father's apparently innocent diversion. Jealousies will be engendered in other families, almost certainly. Scandal may be given—Pharisaic scandal perhaps, but so unnecessary. Duties may be neglected, or at best good work will be left undone.

But it is Father's own unhappiness that concerns us

here. Because, make no mistake about it, this priest will find himself suffering from a restlessness and an inner dissatisfaction that he can't quite put his finger on. Perhaps he doesn't realize it, but he is trying to divide his heart between God and creatures—and in a priest that just can't be successfully done. It is understandable, it is human, for a priest to enjoy being valued and loved as an individual, cherished and ministered to as a friend. But once we have received the Sacrament of Holy Orders, such comforts and consolations must lie outside the range of our vision.

The layman travels to God by one path, the priest by another. For the Christian parent, the joy and the inspiration he finds in his family are an integral part of his vocation, at once a compensation and a help. But the priest has chosen a shorter and a more direct path; for him, any detour must be a dead-end street. The priest must realize that when he made his vow of chastity, he embraced more than mere physical and mental celibacy; he renounced the right to any other comforter but God. Aside from his priest friends and his own immediate family, there is no one to whom the priest has the right of recourse in moments of loneliness and discouragement, except to the One Whom he took as his portion and his inheritance: the God to Whom he has given *all* his heart.

It is evident, I am sure, that this is no contradiction of what I said in the beginning: that basically there is only one kind of spirituality for layman and priest alike. Both are equally obliged to love God supremely; both have the same helps, the same means of grace for the achievement of that end. But each has his own apostolate, his own field of activity. The priest will not fulfill his apostolate by seeking to be, even for a little while, a layman; any more than a layman would fulfill *his* apostolate by neglecting his family to do the work of a priest.

This does not mean that a priest should erect a cold and forbidding barrier between himself and his people. God save us from that! A priest *should* visit his people —but it ought to be a different family or families every day. He should love all his families with an equal love —with the love of Christ. His face should be familiar in every part of his parish; he should be the easily recognized and the easily approached father of all.

As Christ did not disdain to sit at the wedding-feast of Cana, nor at the banquets of Matthew and Simon, so too the priest will sacrifice his own comfort and convenience to bless, by his presence, the wedding breakfasts, the golden- and silver-jubilee dinners, the graduation parties, and the other glad occasions of his flock. It is a fine thing, I think, when a priest can and does enter as fully and as intimately as possible into the life of his people; so long as he shares himself with all alike, and remains ever conscious of his priesthood, of the fact that his heart belongs only to God.

It may seem that I have given a disproportionate amount of space to a problem which to most priests probably is no problem at all. But to the priest who finds that he has, perhaps imperceptibly, become entangled in a network of human affections, the problem can be a very real one. Whether it be this, or some other type of attachment—any division of our heart between God and creatures means that our efficiency as a priest is diminished; our happiness as a priest is marred, if not destroyed. We all need to remind ourselves frequently: "God made us for Himself; no one else will do!"

THE PRAYERFUL PRIEST

TO BE A GOOD PRIEST, primarily it is necessary to be a good man. Sacerdotal sanctity is as simple as that. It is well to remember it, in those moments when Satan cunningly puts into our mind the thought, "Oh, this struggle for virtue is so wearisome! Maybe I should have stayed a layman. I'm sure that I could have been a good layman; but it is so hard to be a good priest."

Jesus was speaking to all of us, priest and layman alike, when He said, "You therefore are to be perfect, even as your heavenly Father is perfect." Jesus did not say, "Thus far shall you go if you are a layman; this much farther must you go if you are a priest." For each of us, priest and layman alike, the sky quite literally is the limit.

It is true that the priest has the obligation to be the pattern for his flock. But the layman is bound to give good example, too. The father who gives scandal to his children is only different in number from the priest who gives scandal to his flock. Good example is obligatory upon all of us; it is not the exclusive province of the priest.

I have in mind a layman of my acquaintance. His wife is in a mental hospital, so he is by necessity bound to a celibate life. This man is at Mass and Holy Communion every morning. He is in his pew several minutes before Mass begins, preparing himself by prayer and recollection for the sacrifice in which he is to have a part. He remains in his pew for several minutes after Mass in devout thanksgiving. He goes to Confession every week, and for him Confession is not a hasty routine. I happen to know that he spends a little time each evening with some solid spiritual reading. What prayers he may say at other times of the day I do not know; but I am confident that he says his Rosary daily, and night and morning prayers at the side of his bed.

Now that doesn't sound like a particularly heroic program, does it? And yet I as a priest would be quite happy if I could be sure that my own spiritual health were as sound as this man's. If he can be as good as he is with a program like that (and there are hundreds of thousands of others like him), then let me not exaggerate the weight of my own obligation to sanctity. Let me not be setting up bogeymen for myself, making holiness seem a more complicated and difficult goal than it is. I have the same means of grace, the same helps that this man has—just let me use them. "Prayer and the sacraments"; those, according to the catechism, are the two wings on which I shall fly to God.

Right now and first of all, let us consider prayer, and the place of prayer in the life of the priest. Do I do as much praying, as effective praying, as a good layman does? Do I begin my day with the sign of the cross, with a "Good morning, God!" the moment I have shut off the alarm? Do I swing out of bed and begin my morning prayers at once, before a single bit of the precious day is wasted? It is a peculiar thing that many priests neglect this basic beginning of a Christian's day: what we might call the standard morning prayers that we learned as a child. Yet, if they are good for the layman, they are good for us. The prayers that we say later on in preparation for Mass will not take their place.

First of all there is the Act of Faith, in which we tell God we believe in Him, and that we believe all that He tells us. Faith, we know, is fundamental to a supernatural life, the kind of life that every Christian is bound to live. We wouldn't *be* Christians, let alone priests, if we didn't believe in God, and if we didn't really believe that He loves us and that He made us for Heaven. Faith is a virtue, and like any virtue it becomes stronger each time we use it, each time we consciously exercise it—just as physical exercise broadens our shoulders and toughens our muscles. So we begin our day by flexing this particular spiritual muscle, as we assert the faith we have and ask for the faith we need.

An act of Faith leads quite naturally to an Act of Hope. If we believe all that God has told us, then of course we are full of hope. God has said that He made us to be happy with Him in Heaven, and that Christ died for our sins, and that He will help us with His grace to come safely to Himself. We find strength and happiness in that thought, and our confidence issues in an Act of Hope. I don't have to point out, surely, how very important this virtue is. If we didn't have a lively and a solid hope of getting to Heaven, none of us would be good for very long, none of us would be priests for very long. If we thought that it was extremely difficult to get to Heaven, if we thought that only great saints could achieve it, if we thought that we had about one chance in a thousand of getting there—well, it would be pretty easy to get discouraged.

What goes on in the mind of a man who abandons his priesthood, I suppose nobody knows except the man himself. Doubtless in some it is a failure in faith, due to an abuse of grace. But I suspect that with some it is a failure in hope; failure perhaps by way of presumption, feeling that somehow, in the end, he will save his soul regardless of what he may do now. In other cases, however, it may be a species of despair: an exaggeration of the difficulties involved and a gross underestimation of the mercy of God.

Actually we know that God wants us in Heaven so much—wants us there even more than we want it ourselves. He tries so hard to steer us towards happiness—happiness here, let it be noted, as well as hereafter. His grace goes before us and follows after; it envelops us like a protective embrace. The fact is we can't *lose* Heaven unless we turn our back on God, as it were, and deliberately walk away from Him; unless we make the decision "I'm going to do the things I want to do, rather than what God wants me to do; Heaven or no Heaven, I am going to go my own way."

God wants us in Heaven so much that, short of taking away our free will, He is going to do everything He can to get us into Heaven. This is what we remember when temptations are strong, when we get discouraged with our own weakness, when the doing of God's Will seems to call for great self-sacrifice. So long as we have this complete trust in God's care for us, this confidence that in the end we shall win through—then we can keep on trying with unflagging determination, no matter what the cost may be. These are the thoughts we have in mind as we make our Act of Hope each morning. We begin the day by giving ourselves a little "toning up," a little boost, a little sharpening for what is ahead of us, with an Act of Hope. We are made for Heaven, and we are on our way there!

And then there naturally will be aroused in any normal human being feelings of love for God Who has loved us so much and Who so continuously has us in His keeping. After all, He didn't even have to make me, in the first place. There were a million, a billion other souls He might have created instead of me. But for some mysterious reason it was *I* that God looked upon and loved, and no one else would do. And so He has given me this chance for the tremendous ecstasy of being with Him forever. He watches over me night and day, so afraid that I might get away from Him, so anxious if I seem to start to wander from Him, almost smothering me with His love, almost drowning me in His grace.

If that sounds too lyrical, really there is hardly any other way we can express, in our inadequate human language, God's attitude towards us. So, unless I am completely callous and insensible to proffered love, this will arouse an answering love in me. The natural thing will be to tell God of my love for Him, to tell Him that I love Him more than anything else or anyone else in the whole wide world which He has created. I shall let nothing come between Him and me. For His sake I shall love my neighbor even as I love myself. I shall love even the people who are hard to love: the rude, the ignorant, the obnoxious. I shall bear my troubles patiently, and I shall be kind to everyone, even to those who may be unkind or hateful towards me. Just as a millionaire will never notice it if he happens to lose a dime, so too it will never bother me unduly if someone does me an injury; I've got so much love from God that the love of other people doesn't matter much. All this is what we mean, when we make our Act of Love.

In the logical order the next step will be to express my gratitude to God. A brand new day opens before me; a new day to live for God, a new day in which to love and serve Him and to grow in holiness. How often · we roll out of bed brown-mouthed and disgruntled. We went to bed late last night and get up weary still. It's raining out. The housekeeper has been in a sulk for a week. We've got a disagreeable interview ahead of us with the parents of the boy we had to expel from school. The church boiler needs repairs—and what's the use of living, anyway? You know the kind of a morning I mean—we all encounter them once in a while.

Well, our Act of Thanksgiving will be a good antidote to such a day. We may start out by saying, "Thank you, dear God, for the new day that You have given me. I pledge myself to try to live it well for You." Then it will be good to go on to mention one or two of the things for which we are especially thankful to God, perhaps mentioning one thing today, another tomorrow, and so on. Today I might thank God for the gift of Faith which He has given me; so many people don't know God, so many don't have the gift of knowing the true Faith which God, without any merit on my part, has given to me. Another time I might thank God for the good parents He gave me, for my brothers and sisters and friends. I might thank Him for my good health, for the gift of sight by which I can see the beauties of His creation and the faces of those I love, the gift of hearing by which I can hear the songs of birds and the beauties of music and the voices of children and baseball broadcasts. I may thank Him for the hands with which I can manipulate knife and fork and camera and golf clubs—the hands in which I can hold His Precious Body and Blood. Above all, and often, I shall thank Him for the priesthood to which He has so undeservedly called me, and for certain specific graces that I can see have been at work in my life. Then of course I shall thank Him for my crosses too; for the opportunity to share a little bit in His sufferings, to make reparation just a little bit for my own sins and for the sins of the world. Oh, there are so many things to thank God for, if only we stop to count our benefits. We shall remember the man who said, "I had no shoes; and I pitied myself until I met a man who had no feet." We shall not be among those who sour their lives and feel sorry for themselves because they have had perhaps one misfortune, the while they forget the thousand good things God has given them.

Then, having made our Act of Thanksgiving in words that should rise naturally to our lips, what comes next? It will be, quite spontaneously, an offering to God of the day for which we have just thanked Him—it will be our Morning Offering. Probably most of us know and use the Morning Offering of the Apostleship of Prayer. It is a fine thing, surely, to unite ourselves with the tens of millions of other members of the Apostleship throughout the world, praying for the special intentions assigned by the Holy Father for this particular month. But whether we use those words or not, the idea is to offer to God, in advance, everything that I do, say, think or suffer in the day that lies ahead. If I say it and *mean* it, then my whole day becomes a prayer: even my most common actions, such as eating my meals, shaving my whiskers, taking my recreation. The work that I do, whatever worries I may have, any disappointments that may come to me—every bit of it becomes a prayer because I have offered it all to God in advance.

There is just one thing we can't offer to God as a gift, just one thing He doesn't want—and that is sin. But, aside from sin, everything in our day, no matter how simple or lowly, no matter how common the action, can be a prayer. This is what it means "to pray always," as both Our Lord and St. Paul have told us we must do. There is just one point to be noted here: someone has rightly observed that the sanctification of our day is not completed by "sprinkling it with holy water" in our Morning Offering. From time to time during the day we should try to recall, for a fleeting instant, that what we are doing we are doing for God; and renew the offering with which our day began.

We come next to the central jewel of all our prayers: the Our Father. When His first priests asked Jesus to teach them to pray, this was His response; so it must be the prayer *par excellence*. But we say it so often that it falls, in so many instances, heedlessly from our lips. Now in our morning prayers, at least once in this day, let us say it slowly, reverently, and thoughtfully. "Hallowed be Thy Name," we say. Is our own love for God obvious to all from the habitual reverence with which we always speak of Him and utter His Holy Name? "Thy Kingdom come." What of our own apostolic spirit? Are we doing our best to extend His Kingdom in our own parish; are we active and generous in our support of the missions, home and foreign? "Thy Will be done." What about our own acceptance of His Will? Did we do any complaining yesterday—about the weather, the food, the bishop, or our bunions?

"Give us this day our daily bread." Are we fully conscious of the "our" in that phrase? We know that we shall not go hungry ourselves. But are we tireless in promoting more frequent Communion in our parish, not scolding but reasoning sweetly and making it as convenient as we can for all to receive who will? Do we sacrifice our own convenience to take Holy Communion frequently to the sick and invalid? Do we share of our own abundance with the poor—not only in our own parish but in the world at large through the St. Vincent de Paul Society, the Bishops' Relief Collection, the Pope's Collection, and similar agencies?

"Forgive us our trespasses." Are we sure, as we say that, that there isn't even the tiniest bit of bitterness or resentment in our heart against anybody at all—against our assistant, or our pastor, or our neighboring pastor, or some obstreperous family in the parish? "Lead us not into temptation." Are we co-operating with God on that—are we certain, as we say it, that there isn't any voluntary occasion of sin in our lives, no person or attachment whose danger we try studiously to ignore and are reluctant to give up? "Deliver us from all evil." Indeed yes; from *all* evil. From the evil of wasted time and uncharitable talk and careless prayer and petty vanity and all the rest.

Just once a day let us say the Our Father thoughtfully, like this. Then, while we are still shaking our head at the thought of our own frailty we shall think, as a needy son always does think, of our Mother. After

Our Lord's prayer will come the prayer dictated by God and spoken by the angel: the Hail Mary. Again, this too is a prayer whose beauty has been filmed over by so much repetition. Let us savor it at least this once in the day, as we confide the day's responsibilities and cares, the day's weaknesses and dangers, to the loving hands of her whose sons we are. And let every fiber of our being be in it as we beg her to "pray for us sinners now (*now*, NOW) and at the hour of our death"— that supremely crucial hour.

We shall do well to conclude our morning prayers (or perhaps we should have begun them) with a renewal of our intention to gain all the indulgences that we can, this day. We know that to gain an indulgence it is sufficient to have an habitual intention; we know that to keep the intention habitual it should be renewed from time to time. All through the day we shall be saying prayers to which indulgences are attached: our Rosary, our breviary, our table prayers, and doubtless many others. There will be many days when, because of our membership in some pious association or confraternity, we shall be entitled to a plenary indulgence just by the fact of having celebrated Mass. In many cases we shall not advert to the indulgence; but if we have our intention at the beginning of the day, not one of the indulgences will be lost to us or to the Suffering Souls.

There is another prayer that ought to be in the orisons of every priest. We may wish to fit it in here, or into our thanksgiving after Mass, or as an addendum to our Rosary: that is the Litany of the Sacred Heart of Jesus. We recall that one of the promises made by Our Lord to St. Margaret Mary was that He would give to priests who would have a special devotion to His Sacred Heart the power to touch souls and to win over even the most hardened sinners. A priest hardly dares to ignore a pledge like that. Somewhere, surely, we shall find a place for the Litany of the Sacred Heart, or for *some* prayer in honor of the Sacred Heart.

Perhaps some may think it surprising that I should, in addressing myself to brother priests, devote so much space to so elementary a matter as morning prayers. Yet it is possible that in those examinations of our spiritual life which we do make from time to time, we may concentrate our attention on the superstructure to the neglect of the foundation. Our Lord did not intend to make the acquisition of sanctity an elaborate and confusing affair. For the secular priest in particular, whose only cloister is the bathroom and for whom no such thing as a real schedule can exist, the fundamental Christian duties must be his principal path to holiness. They will be, too, if he fulfills them well. Prayer is a lifting of the mind and heart to God. Morning prayer is not the whole of the story by any means. But if we do lift our hearts and our minds stoutly and generously to God in the morning, there is a good chance that they will stay there the rest of the day. If we have started our day well as simple Christians, we have started our day well as priests.

THE PERSEVERING PRIEST

IN EVERY PRIESTS' retreat there are two topics that are certain to come up for discussion: the Divine Office and meditation. This inevitable recurrence is a pretty reliable indication that Office and meditation are constant and stubborn problems in a priest's spiritual life.

Most of us probably don't need that proof. We have learned through the years, through a long chain of resolutions made and broken, how hard it is to pray our breviary well, how hard it is to make a daily meditation.

We might consider the Divine Office first. This is one obligation that is distinctly ours, one that we do not share with the laity. The layman (I speak of one who aims at more than mediocrity) should pray morning and night; so should we. He should try to make God's Will his supreme guide, and live his day for God; so should we. He should make daily Mass and Communion a part of his program when possible; so should we. He should receive the Sacrament of Penance bi-monthly at least; so should we. He should find some time for meditation; so should we.

In other words, the means of grace that make for a

good *Christian* life are the same means of grace that make for a good *priestly* life—with this one exception. The burden (if we want to call it that) of the breviary is distinctly ours. I say, "if we want to call it that." Maybe we don't *want* to call the breviary a burden; but in practice we often feel that it is, and we may as well be honest enough to admit it, so that we can discover the reason for it and maybe do something about it.

It helps to clarify things if we bear in mind that the Divine Office has two aspects, two values: that of personal prayer and that of official function. It is in its character of personal prayer that the breviary is most likely to seem burdensome, even to priests who value prayer and are conscientious about prayer. The reason is obvious: it just isn't natural to man to pray in an alien tongue. The ease with which we establish communication with God is in proportion to the care we take in removing obstacles to that communication: the moral obstacles of sin and self-attachment, and physical obstacles such as noise or other activities which compete for our attention.

There is no evading the fact that an unfamiliar language must be classified as one of these physical obstacles. Prayer is defined as the raising of the mind and heart to God. Except in the prayer of pure contemplation, that means that the mind is at work; lovingly at work, but still at work. That means that the mind must have words to work with, since there is no thought without the *verbum mentis*. That means that much spontaneity in prayer is lost if the mind has to labor through the mechanics of translation. Perhaps there are linguistic

c

scholars who can think in Latin as readily as in their native tongue; but we know that by and large the priesthood is not made up of linguistic scholars.

It is useful, I think, to face frankly this barrier of language in the Divine Office, for two reasons. First, it may move us to pray for the removal of the barrier. It is quite legitimate to wish for the privilege of praying our breviary in the vernacular; it is quite legitimate to advocate such a change; it is quite legitimate and even praiseworthy to pray for such a consummation—so long as all this is done within the framework of complete obedience and submission to the judgment of the Holy See. There is nothing sacred about Latin *per se*. In St. Benedict's day Latin was the language of the people. It was easy for St. Benedict to speak stirringly about the *Opus Dei* to his monks; they were praying in their native tongue. It is not quite so easy for us to distinguish between the *Opus Dei* and the *Onus diei;* to speak in stirring accents of this Work of God. For my own part, I pray for the day when the breviary may be for us a book of personal prayer as well as an official priestly function; for the day when we can speak God's praises easily and joyfully in our own language. Meanwhile we shall leave the outcome of our prayers in the hands of God and submit our own judgment to that of Christ in His Church.

Of course, even were our breviary in English, that alone would not be a guarantee that we would say it well. Even though it is easier to be distracted in Latin, it still is not too difficult to be distracted in English; which brings us to the second point worth considering in connection with this barrier of language: the doubly urgent need to *begin* well, as we settle to the recitation of our breviary.

Distractions in prayer are inevitable, the human mind being the capricious faculty that it is. We should be doing ourselves a great disservice if we thought that we were miserable failures at prayer, simply because our mind keeps wandering all over creation when we try to pray. And we should be involving ourselves in needless frustration if we kept going back and repeating prayers that were said with an absent mind. The cure for distractions does not lie in repetition. "That way lies madness," as the dramatist might put it.

Anyone could pray well if it were easy to pray; the harder it is for us to pray, the more merit there is in our prayer. We have told that to others often enough; we need only to apply it ourselves. If we have settled to our prayer in a *spirit* of prayer; that is, if we have put aside unnecessary exterior distractions; if we have placed ourselves mentally in the presence of God and made an advance offering of our prayer to God, including its imperfections and distractions; if we have formed the intention for which we wish to offer our prayer (and a special intention for each hour of the breviary is a helpful practice)—then our prayer will be a good and an efficacious prayer. The value of our breviary as *personal* prayer must lie largely in this *spirit* of prayer, since the Latin will limit the help we might otherwise get from the thoughts and ideas of the Office itself.

However, we know that our breviary is more than a personal prayer. It is also, and I suppose we might say mainly, an official function of our priesthood. We have been designated by the Church, the *ecclesia orans*, to be her official mouthpieces in offering honor to God. The Church, the Mystical Body of Christ, is praying through us. It is this above all else that gives value to the recitation of the Divine Office by those in major orders or in solemn vows. If you understand that I am using the term in a broad sense, I might say that there is an *ex opere operato* effect, as the Church makes use of us to address her Spouse. So long as we have brought to the recitation of our office a decent reverence and such attention as we can, then we shall have performed our duty well.

And now, what about mental prayer? That *is* a perennial problem for most of us. Not for all of us, I know. There are priests who have persevered valiantly in their fixed period of daily meditation ever since they left the seminary. But I doubt whether such priests constitute the majority. This doesn't mean that most priests do not meditate. I think that most priests meditate far more than they themselves realize. Whenever we read an article in a clerical magazine or a review about some phase of priestly life or work, and compare ourselves with the ideal proposed there and decide to do something about it, we have meditated. Whenever we examine our conscience and note our shortcomings and resolve upon a change for the future, we have meditated. Whenever we read a spiritual book and apply to ourselves the truths discussed there, we have meditated. Whenever we pray our Rosary, we have meditated. Whenever, in our Mass preparation or thanksgiving, we think of what imperfect men we are, and pray for the grace to acquire the virtue we are most lacking in, we have meditated. I don't think that many of us get through any day without having meditated at least a little. If we didn't, we would not be the priests that we are, even admitting all our imperfections.

The same thing is true of mental prayer in general. (Meditation, as we know, is only one form of mental prayer.) Since all prayer is a raising of the mind and heart to God, we know that there must be recollection and love in every prayer, including vocal prayer. When, however, without any set formula of words, our mind turns to God, to our Lord Jesus Christ, with any movement of the will—such as sentiments of loyalty, or sorrow for sin, or gratitude, or sense of dependence—then we have practiced mental prayer. Like meditation, this too may happen oftener than we give ourselves credit for: it happens while we distribute Holy Communion, or sit in the confessional, or at the scamnum while the choir sings the Gloria or Credo; while we are on a sick call, or preparing a sermon, or while we are falling asleep at night.

The Code of Canon Law in Canon 125 directs the Ordinary to see to it that his priests spend some time every day in mental prayer. It may seem a rather impractical Canon, since it would be pretty difficult for any bishop to police the consciences of his priests. But certainly an Ordinary would have much cause for worry if he did know of any priest in his diocese who gave no more time to prayer than that required for the hurried and routine recitation of his Office and for the casual and mechanical celebration of Mass. But I don't think that the bishop would have to worry about such a man very long; because in all probability he would not be very long in the priesthood—not, that is, in the active care of souls.

Granting, then, that every good priest does practice mental prayer and meditation, however haphazard that practice may be, let us grant also that none of us is achieving the degree of sanctity that God wants and the world needs. We may not, we *must* not, be content to remain merely good priests. "There is but one sadness," says the French writer Léon Bloy, "and that is for us not to be saints." We must keep alive in ourselves that smoldering sense of dissatisfaction with ourselves as we are. Ours must be the happy unhappiness of one who knows that there still is much to be done—with the confidence that, God's grace assisting, he can do it. In our spiritual life there can never be the joy of fruition, the satisfaction of a job that is finished and done.

However, this holy discontent which every good priest experiences cannot be indefinitely satisfied with a vague purpose to do something about it in the hazy future. Unless our discontent is fed with the fuel of honest effort, it finds its death eventually in a sterile tepidity—or it leads to that state of chronic discouragement which makes many a good priest so unaccountably miserable. Just as husband and wife cannot go on continuously frustrating the procreative act without severe emotional damage to themselves, so neither can we forever checkmate our vocation to sanctity without grave harm to our spiritual fabric.

In other words, the irregular and fitful mental prayer which admittedly is a part of any good priest's day needs to be implemented by daily and methodical meditation. When I say "methodical" I am not referring to any particular *pattern* of meditation, such as the Ignatian method or the Sulpician method. Such scientific dissection of the meditative process is fine if you have mastered it, can use it, and find it helpful. But I think that some are confused and hindered, rather than aided, by trying to adhere to a set formula. So when I speak of "methodical" meditation I mean only the method involved in having a fixed hour and place for our meditation, so that we establish a *habit* of meditation. It takes a little while to establish such a habit; but once we have done so, our meditation becomes as natural a part of our day as our meals, our breviary, or our post-prandial nap.

And let's not magnify the difficulties of meditation. Let's not take refuge in the specious alibi that we "just can't meditate"; that we "just aren't the meditating kind." What's so esoteric about meditation? If we can look in a mirror and say "I need a shave" and then get out our razor, we can equally well look into the mirror of God's truth and say "Here's something that needs correcting" and proceed to do something about it. That really is all there is to meditation.

If we have the *will* to meditate, then all we need in addition is a chair and a book; and of course the time set aside for it. The ideal time for our meditation is in the morning before our Mass, and the ideal place is in church before the Blessed Sacrament. But we may as well be realistic about these things. Meditation before Mass means getting up half an hour earlier. If our work keeps us up far into the evening, it may well be that with all the good will in the world we just can't seem to get going in the morning. I think that it is much better to make a meditation before supper or before going to bed, and to do it every day, than to *say* we will do it in the morning and then actually do it about once a week, or maybe give up entirely.

The same thing is true of making our meditation in

church. We have to be honest with ourselves in measuring our own capacity, in facing up squarely to what we can expect of ourselves. If the extra effort involved in getting over to church is likely to make us miss our meditation, but we would meditate if the book were right there by the easy chair in our study, then let it be the study. The essence of meditation does not lie in the time or the place. Once we have got into the habit of meditating, the external accidentals will perfect themselves as we go along.

Let's be realistic too about the book we use. It should be a book that is meaty enough for our needs, a book that will make us think; but it need not be a book that was specifically designed for meditation. The book-review section of the clerical reviews will be a good guide to us in the selection of our books—although tastes differ so much that a book review sometimes can be a misleading guide. If we buy a book and then find that it does not hold our interest or that it is insipid to our taste—well, let's not keep using it just because we have three dollars invested in it. Our meditation time is too precious for parsimony. Let's cut our losses and try another book. Or if we are economy-minded, perhaps we can browse through the library of a priest friend and find a book suited to our needs, something that our friend has tried and found substantial.

I said that all that is needed for our meditation is a chair and a book. There is one other small piece of equipment that I myself find helpful, and that is a pencil. A pencil in my hand seems to put me a little more on the alert. Because the pencil seems to beg for something to underline, I watch more closely for thoughts that will strike home. When the pencil has done its work, I stop and think a bit about the sentence I have marked. I do not worry about how many pages or how many paragraphs I may cover; when the time is up that I have set aside for my meditation, I close the book until tomorrow.

This is a very rudimentary sort of meditation, I know. It really is nothing more than a ruminative sort of spiritual reading. But even this, if we have begun by placing ourselves in the presence of God, with a quick plea for His light upon our reflections—even this can help a lot. Those who are of a more contemplative nature, or perhaps are more generous in their mortifications than myself, doubtless would pass very quickly from this to a higher and less pedestrian form of prayer. But I think that the legislator of Canon 125 would gladly settle for this. And those of us who may have found daily meditation to be a constantly recurring problem—who may perhaps have magnified the difficulties in their own minds—may find courage in this simplicity. Surely it is not a mystic experience beyond the reach of anyone.

Canon 125 mentions another spiritual duty which is, I suspect, the object of frequently renewed resolutions on the part of many of us—that is, our daily visit to Jesus in the Blessed Sacrament. It is not through cold indifference that we fail in this duty. We are quite aware of the fact that it is for our Lord Jesus Christ that we are working, in His interests that we labor. We know that a few extra moments spent in quiet communion with Him each day can double our effectiveness as priests, can correct our errors and comfort us in our failures. But in parochial work our schedule is so irregular, our day so crowded, that sometimes it seems awfully hard to make those few steps from rectory to sacristy. I know that it has been so with me. And yet I must make a con-

fession: there have been times when I have been too busy
to pay a visit to church, but nevertheless have found
time to drive a mile for a supply of cigarettes. Again it
is a matter of establishing the habit, so that something
seems missing from the day in which there has been no
courtesy call upon our Master. The essential start would
be to choose a time, again realistically, when we know
that we can spend at least five minutes alone with Jesus.
If the time is after lunch or after dinner, I don't think
that a caller waiting for us in our office would object
if we told him, "Excuse me, I'll be right back, but I
have to go over to church for a couple of minutes."

Whether it is a matter of the Divine Office, or of meditation, or of visit to the Blessed Sacrament, what we
must as priests—indeed, as *Christians*—preserve at all
costs is our spirit of prayer. It is only a spirit of prayer
that will keep our zeal from sagging and stagnating. It
is only a spirit of prayer that will keep us mindful,
through good days and bad, that it is for God that we
live and for God that we labor. He does not need us,
but we do need Him. All our cleverness and our sweat
will be wasted—we shall come to the end of our day
empty-handed, like a farmer who carries home a sack
of wheat with a tear in the bottom of the sack—if the
power of prayer does not continually mend the holes
that self keeps punching in the best of our works.

The one encouraging thing is that we do keep trying,
most of us. We resolve and we fail and we resolve
again. It might seem ridiculous to some that a priest,
after ten or twenty or thirty years, should still be renewing and repairing the resolutions that he made in the
first year of his priesthood. But that very spirit of perse-
verance is itself a grace of God: that dogged, will-not-

be-defeated determination that *this* time we can and will do better. Once we have lost that, then *all* is lost. The priest who has grown cynical or discouraged, the priest who can no longer summon the will to make new resolutions, the priest whose answer is *"cui bono?"* to every impulse of grace: that priest needs desperately to cry out with all his heart as he begins each hour of his Office: *"Domine, ad adjuvandum me festina!"*

THE SACRIFICING PRIEST

MOST OF US are likely to feel a bit miffed if someone refers to us as a "preacher" or a "minister." We have a right to feel slighted by such an appellation. It does belittle us by denying or ignoring our most glorious prerogative. We *are* preachers, true enough, if we do our duty and expound the Gospel each Sunday. We *are* ministers, too, since the word means servant, and we serve in Christ's Name the souls entrusted to us.

But we are far more than preacher or minister. Besides speaking from the pulpit and serving our flock in lesser ways, we offer sacrifice in Christ's Name—the Holy Sacrifice of the Mass. Because we offer sacrifice we are called priests—the only word which accurately describes what we are, "offerers of sacrifice."

When a Protestant man is ordained a minister, it simply means that he is officially delegated by his particular Church to preach the Gospel and to be in charge of a congregation. No change takes place in the man; he receives no power that he did not have before. But when a Catholic man receives the Sacrament of Holy Orders, a great change does take place. There is imparted to him a most wonderful power which he did not have before:

the power to change bread and wine into Christ's own Body and Blood; the power to speak the words by which the Redeemer, over and over again, will renew the offering of Himself upon the Cross to God the Father. *That* is the power that makes us priests.

It is easy for us to forget the grandeur of our state, our historical closeness to Christ, the directness of the line of our descent from him. We know what importance the world attaches (snobbishly, perhaps) to lineal descent from some great historical personage. There may be a bum living down by the railroad tracks, scavenging for his food in the garbage cans. Yet if he can prove that he is a direct descendant of, let us say King Henry VIII, he immediately becomes a newsworthy figure.

Each of us today, if he had the time and money necessary for the investigation, could trace his priesthood right back to Christ. Here is a Father Gallagher, for example, who was ordained a priest in 1950 by a Bishop O'Brien. Bishop O'Brien was consecrated bishop in 1910 by Bishop Meyers. Bishop Meyers was consecrated in 1880 by Bishop Chaillon. Our imaginary Father Gallagher would travel from city to city, visiting the chancery offices, looking up the documents. Eventually he would come to Archbishop Carroll of Baltimore, the first bishop in the United States, who himself was consecrated in England. Our investigator then would have to cross the ocean to continue his research. In England, going back from bishop to bishop, he would come in time to St. Augustine of Canterbury who was consecrated bishop by Pope St. Gregory in the sixth century. On to Rome then our fictional priest would go, to trace his priesthood back to Peter himself, and through Peter to Jesus Christ.

All this is theoretical, of course. Actually in the course

of nineteen hundred years there have been fires and floods, wars and disasters. Many of the documents long since have perished, and perhaps in the beginning there weren't any documents. But it does bring home to us the fact that the power of the priesthood has been transmitted in a direct and continuous line from Christ, through His apostles, to us who are marked with the priestly character today. Like a golden chain running through the beads of a rosary, the Sacrament of Holy Orders links together each successive generation of bishops and priests, links us all together with Christ. In embryo, we might say, each of us was present at the Last Supper. As Jesus spoke the words which made His apostles priests, He was seeing in His divine Mind not only them; He was looking down through time, He was seeing you and me, as He said, "Do this in remembrance of Me!"

The mystery that I most look forward to seeing resolved when (*Seipso adjuvante!*) I see God face to face in Heaven is not one of the Great Mysteries such as that of the Blessed Trinity, or the Hypostatic Union, or the interaction of grace and free will, I feel no urgency to know the answer to those. What I would like to know is why Jesus Christ ever picked me for His priesthood. Out of all the millions who certainly were more worthy and who surely would have served Him better, why did He put His finger upon me? Knowing ourselves as we do (I am sure that each of us has felt this), to think that Christ has made us such intimates of Himself, such close colleagues in His work of salvation! It is almost enough to shake our faith, isn't it?

If we happened to see a sculptor of international fame expending infinite pains in fashioning a beautiful work of art out of a block of unsubstantial snow, we should be moved to cry out, "What a pity to waste such talent on such inferior material." That is about the way we feel as we think of Christ fashioning us in His own image through the character of Holy Orders. Almost we are tempted to exclaim, "What a waste, that such power and such grace be entrusted to such a wobbly mediocrity as myself!"

But breast-beating will get us nowhere. So we jump quickly and logically to the question: "How am I using this incredible power that has been conferred upon me? What am I doing to make my identification with Christ as complete on my part as it is on His? What am I doing to reduce to a minimum the friction, the resistance, which His divine action must encounter as it works in me and through me?" In other words, what of my Mass?

In discussing here the Mass, I should like to do so from an ascetical rather than a dogmatic point of view. Without belittling the value and importance to a priest of a sound knowledge of the theology of the Mass, I think that we can pass over, for our purpose, such metaphysical questions (still debated by theologians) as the manner and the degree in which the scientific concept of sacrifice is realized in the Mass. For the assaying of our own part in the Mass, it is enough to say that in the Mass Christ is renewing the offering to God the Father of His infinite love, incarnated in the infinitely perfect obedience of His life and death, in the infinitely unrestrained *giving* of Himself which culminated on Calvary.

The Mass then is the renewal, the re-offering, the re-giving for our sakes, of the infinitely perfect gift of love which Christ made once for all on the cross. And in the Mass Christ offers not only His own love to the Father, but also the love of all who unite themselves with Christ in the offering of the Mass. As the lesser is absorbed into the greater, so is this human love of ours, imperfect and insignificant in itself, absorbed into and transformed by Christ's own love, made a part of the total love, the one and single gift which He is offering.

This participation in the Mass is the privilege of all Christians. But, because of his special relationship to Christ, it is pre-eminently the privilege of the priest. Because we are skirting the dogmatic side of the Mass, we can leave aside here discussion of the additional fruit —what theologians call the *special* fruit—which accrues to the Church and the faithful from the personal holiness of the celebrant. What interests us right now as priests is what the Mass should and can mean to *us*.

Granting that the gift which Jesus is offering in the Mass to the Father is a gift of love, it follows that our own participation in the Mass will be more perfect, to the degree that the love we bring to the Mass is a genuine love. Our union with Christ in the Mass will be more complete to the extent that our spirit of self-immolation is more total. Love, we know, expresses itself, proves itself, by *giving*. The more plenary is our desire and intention to give of ourselves to God, the closer is our identification with the sacrificing Christ.

The ideal state of mind and will then, with which to begin and to offer our Mass, is one of selfless desire to do God's Will as perfectly as we can. The feeling that should be in our heart, especially as we approach the Consecration, should be something like this: "Dear Jesus, take my love and unite it with Thine; with Thine offer it to our Father. Help me to do His Will always. I don't care whether it means sickness and suffering; I don't care whether it means failure and humiliation. Anything I've got I'm ready to give up in a minute if You want me to, if it is not in accord with Your Will. Any plans or preferences that I may have, no matter how dear to me, I want You to smash them to bits if they run counter to what You know is best. Do what You want with me dear Jesus, do what You want with me; I have no other desire but to be wholly Yours."

Those words will not be on our lips, of course; the words on our lips must be the words of the Mass itself. The sentiments may not even be explicitly in our consciousness throughout the Mass. I know by experience how easy it is for the human mind to wander, even at the tremendous moment of Transubstantiation. But this should be our virtual intention throughout the Mass. It will not be our virtual intention *in* the Mass unless it is our habitual intention outside the Mass—and that is not easy. The words are easy to say—but to make the words a reality by a corresponding actuality behind the words —that is not so easy.

When we have a pet project under way, for example —something that we've put a lot of time and sweat and maybe money into, something that is going to mean a lot of satisfaction and happiness to us in one way or another—to preserve—even while we are knocking ourselves out on the thing—to preserve this attitude: "God, sweep it all away if You want to," isn't easy. Because it is not merely a phlegmatic resignation to God's Will that we are aiming at, not merely a stoic acceptance of the ills of life. We are aiming at an habitual attitude of *attachment* to God's Will, a permanent "fix" on God's Will, a loving and a joyous *embracing* of His Will. This isn't easy. It takes a lot of prayer; it takes a lot of grace.

The prayer for it we put into our Mass; the grace for it flows from our Mass. This indeed is the principal personal fruit of the Mass for the priest who tries to unite himself wholly with Christ in the Mass. Hesitantly, imperfectly, almost ashamedly, we unite our shabby gift of love with that of Christ; assimilating it to His own, He carries it to God the Father. Back to us through the hands of Christ, nay in the very Person of Christ in Communion, comes the Father's gift to us: an increase in love for Him, a greater adaptability to His Will, a greater sensitivity to the motions of His Spirit. And so the holy wheel revolves, in our Masses day by day; our weakling love ascending to God; a purified and strengthened love coming back to us.

The greater part of our immediate preparation for Mass, I feel sure, should be given to the effort to form within ourselves, in realistic and articulate fashion, this attitude of self-giving. That is why it is such a loss and a tragedy to ascend to the altar with inadequate preparation, such as the rapid recitation of a few formalized Latin prayers; or what is worse, to begin our Mass with no preparation at all, depending on the brief moments of the "Mementos" to make our intentions and to direct our wills—only to find, perhaps, that even the "Memento" has gone by in distraction and inattention.

One of the most pitiable of creatures, I think, is the priest who has let his Mass become just a routine part of his day's work. Because the Mass is our whole life! Take everything else away from us, and we still are priests. Our Mass, fruitfully celebrated, will accomplish far more for us, for our parish, for the Church, than all the cleverness and ambition and energy that we can pour into the rest of the day. There just is no possibility of putting it too strongly—the need for a thoughtful and prayerful preparation for Mass. We have said our prayers at our bedside; good! We have spent some time on our daily meditation; splendid! But for those last two or three minutes before we begin to vest, let us at our *prie-dieu* summon all our spiritual resources to recall what we are about to do and to make a genuine act of self-immolation in union with Christ. Perhaps I am rash to say so, who myself have yet so much to learn and so far to go; but I do feel that there is nothing else that can be said about the Mass, nothing else that can be done about the Mass, that equals in importance this preparation, this uniting of our will with that of Christ, so that we may bring a fitting gift to the altar.

There *are* other things that can be said about the Mass, of course. It can be pointed out that our love for our Mass and the degree of recollection we bring to our Mass will reflect itself in the manner in which we offer Mass. This means that we shall celebrate the Holy Mysteries unhurriedly, with deliberateness and reverence. What *is* the hurry, anyway? What is coming after Mass that will be more important than the Mass itself?

It means that we shall be careful to articulate well the prayers of the Mass. The secret prayers will be said as they are supposed to be said, not silently but in a voice that is audible to ourselves. The low-voice prayers will be said so that the servers at least can hear us. The *clara-voce* prayers will be said so that those in the front pews and beyond can hear us—hear not merely a jumbled rumble or rattle but enunciated words that they could understand if they knew Latin well enough. This is something on which all of us have need of a careful periodic check-up. It is so easy, repeating the same words day after day, to grow slovenly in the formation of our syllables, to slur and elide and swallow until the angels themselves would find it hard to understand us. A simple way to make the check-up on ourselves is to take the missal (outside of Mass, of course) and read aloud some of the familiar prayers—the *Communicantes*, for example, the *Lavabo*, the Last Gospel—with reasonable rapidity but *very* distinctly. If we find that we stutter and stumble, then we can be very sure that in the Mass itself we are mutilating many of the familiar prayers.

Love for our Mass will dictate too that we be attentive to the ceremonies of the Mass: attentive to the bows—slight, medium or profound, as the rubrics may specify; attentive to the position of the hands—folded, extended, or upon the altar, as the case may be (have you ever noticed the rather surprising variance among priests in the simple matter of extending the hands?); attention to the genuflections, touching the knee to the floor, barring infirmity; attention to the eyes, keeping them cast down when we face the congregation, as called for by the rubrics.

In practice, however, it isn't the inaccuracy of the minor ceremonies that needs emphasis so much as it is the tendency to slovenliness—which in turn can be traced to those twin enemies of reverent celebration: familiarity and haste. There is the zip-zip of the hand over the *oblata* that looks more like an attack of the palsy than it looks like the sign of the cross. There is the flip-flap of the hand that tries to touch forehead, breast, and shoulders at one and the same time, and is a travesty of the *signum crucis.* There is the jet-propelled turn, from book to center to people and back again, while the candles all but waver in the breeze of the passing. Most of us have had the experience at some time of assisting at the Mass of another priest, when we have been tempted to cry out: "Father, take it easy! What are you running from? The church isn't on fire!" He probably was a very good priest, too, because no priest does this intentionally. If the hasty, choppy, jerky priest could see a movie of himself in the act of saying Mass, he probably would swear that it was trick photography; at extra-fast speed; he wouldn't believe that it could be he that skittered so through the Holy Sacrifice.

We may have the gift of tongues and the precision of movement which enable us to offer our Mass with absolute correctness and still with great dispatch. We still have the obligation to celebrate the Mysteries with a deliberation and a visible reverence that our people can perceive and profit by. It is not hypocrisy to slow ourselves deliberately for the sake of our people. We are hypocrites if we do something publicly and insincerely to gain a reputation of sanctity for ourselves. But when we do something publicly as a help and an encouragement to others, we are giving edification. And who will deny our obligation to edify, to build up the faith of the members of the Mystical Body? I do not mean that we should dawdle over our Mass—still less do I mean that there should be any affectation or dramatization to our words and gestures. That one word "reverent" will cover the situation perfectly; it is the golden mean between hastiness and pokiness.

Sometimes a priest will blame his people for his hurriedness at Mass. "If I don't hustle through Mass," he will say, "my people will stop coming." Such an alibi is a rank injustice to our laity. I have seen more people coming late to Mass, leaving early from Mass, and gazing around during Mass, in those churches where the Mass was hurried through, than I have seen in churches where the Mass was offered with evident faith and devotion on the part of the celebrant. I have never heard, nor have you, of anyone who ever drifted away from the Faith because Mass was too long; but I am sure that if we dug a bit, we could find fallen-away Catholics whose lapse began with a disesteem for the Mass caused by the streamlined speed of the Masses they attended.

If we have prepared well for our Mass, if we have offered our Mass well, in a spirit of self-immolation, co-victims with Christ (distractions or no!), then we shall want to consolidate our spiritual gains by a few minutes of earnest thanksgiving. It doesn't take long to kneel in the sanctuary to thank Jesus again for the immeasurable privilege that has been ours, to beg Him to remain with us throughout the day, so that we can carry out in deed the full *giving* of ourselves that was our spirit in the Mass; to recite the *"Trium puerorum"*—the prayer of praise and adoration which is a forecast of our eternal occupation in Heaven; and to end with the indulgenced prayer before the crucifix. (Incidentally, the *"Trium puerorum,"* which has a sacramental efficacy as a thanksgiving prayer because it is prescribed by the Church, need not be recited in Latin unless we so prefer. My own choice is to use English in my prayers whenever I can. I think it might encourage better thanksgivings after Mass if the prayer-cards found in most sacristies were in the vernacular rather than in Latin.) And if I may venture the suggestion: if someone comes into the sacristy to see us on a bit of business as we are divesting, that person will not feel offended if we say, "Excuse me for just three minutes while I make a little thanksgiving." No Catholic minds taking second place to God.

Well, if we can examine our consciences on these four points: our preparation for Mass, our recollection and devotion during Mass, our external reverence in celebrating Mass, our intense (even though brief) thanksgiving after Mass; if we can examine our consciences without having to say, "*Mea culpa, mea culpa*"—then indeed are we truly priests, worthy ministers of the altar, after the sacrificial Heart of Christ.

THE DISSATISFIED PRIEST

AMONG THE MANY intriguing bits of phenomena which make up the so-called American Way of Life are the institutions known as Schools for Models. In such a school, a girl whose ambition it is to become a professional model can supposedly receive the training she needs in order to appear successfully on a mannequin's platform or a magazine cover. At first hand I know no more about such schools than does any other priest. But by hearsay I understand that new pupils at such academies very frequently are surprised and disappointed at the nature of their first lessons. The neophyte expects to begin by learning how to arrange a beautiful hair-do for herself, how to make up her face to best advantage, how to smile charmingly. Instead, she finds that she has to learn how to sit, how to stand, how to walk. If she pouts that she already knows how to sit and stand and walk, that she has been doing these things all her life, then her teacher doubtless will point out that there is a right way and a wrong way of doing these things. The teacher will proceed to show the pupil what is wrong with her posture and her movements; day after day the pupil will practice doing these things in the approved manner.

If I may be permitted the well-known ascent from the ridiculous to the sublime, I should like to recall that we priests are attending a school for models, a school that never dismisses, that never ends. We have undertaken to model our lives upon that of Jesus Christ, so that Christ can make Himself visible in the world in the only way that is open to Him—through us. We may feel—perhaps with some justification—that we aren't doing too bad a job of it. Our Mass is offered reverently and is linked with a proper preparation and an adequate thanksgiving. Our Divine Office is recited with a fair degree of recollection. We never miss our Rosary, and we do get in a bit of spiritual reading and mental prayer each day. Not perfect, maybe, but then who is?

No one is, of course. But if ever we are tempted to this feeling of self-satisfaction, it will mean that we haven't taken a good square look at ourselves for some time. We haven't been actually comparing ourselves, and the way we live, with Jesus and the way He would live if He were in our shoes. And we never shall make much progress in the School of Christ unless we keep seriously at the business of making ourselves over. It is in our daily Particular Examen, especially, that this work of revision to the image of Christ is accomplished.

Perhaps it is too general a statement that I make; but I suspect that there is no other spiritual exercise, basic to growth in holiness, so often and so much neglected by us diocesan priests as the Particular Examen. We made it in the seminary (at least we were present for it) because the bell gave the signal and we trooped dutifully to chapel or prayer-hall. But would it be an exaggeration to say that most of us now would hate to be queried on our fidelity to the practice of Particular Examen since leaving the seminary? I know that I myself would shrink from such an accounting. Yet all the great luminaries of asceticism, all the masters of the spiritual life, say that the Examen is fundamental to spiritual advancement. Either they are wrong in saying so, or we are wrong in not doing it. I fear that the fault lies with us.

Even without the consensus of tradition, reason alone would tell us of the importance of the Particular Examen, whether we called it by that name or not. We know that growth in holiness is normally a slow and gradual process (I say *normally*, because no one can limit God's grace to rigid rules). We develop spiritually very much as we develop physically; virtue is strengthened by repeated acts, as muscles are toughened by repeated use; one virtue is added to another, as new cell unites to the old. Barring God's very special intervention, a person does not suddenly become a saint by a single act of the will; we do not even acquire a single virtue by one act of the will. It is by repetition: exercising the same virtue (in the beginning perhaps painfully and with difficulty) over and over again, that the virtue becomes a solidly established part of our character.

It is at this gradual, steady growth that the Particular Examen aims. It is a form of scrutiny which differs greatly from the ordinary "examination of conscience." The examination of conscience that we make preparatory to Confession is a general survey of the time that has elapsed since our last Confession; we run through the week or weeks to see what sins we have committed and how often, so that we can give a lucid account to our confessor. Then there is the examination of conscience that we usually make as part of our night prayers, just before reciting our Act of Contrition. This again is an all-inclusive glance over the day that is past, to recall and to include in our sorrow any failures there may have been during the day.

The Particular Examen is different from either of these examinations of conscience. Its purpose is not to count up our sins, but to overcome our faults one by one, and to implant one by one the corresponding virtues in which we are lacking. The two things—the elimination of a fault and the acquisition of a virtue—go hand in hand. A fault is simply the hole in the ground which disappears when you shovel in the earth. In the abstract it may be possible to conceive of someone who lacks a certain fault without possessing the corresponding virtue; but not in practice. You cannot overcome pride without becoming humble; and obversely you cannot become unselfish without selfishness disappearing.

We all know that there is a difference between a fault and a sin. (I suppose that "vice" would be a more accurate term, theologically speaking, than "fault"; but "vice" today has too many shades of meaning.) In any case, a fault is a basic weakness, a "weak streak" in me that will cause me to commit certain kinds of sins. The fault is still there, even when the sin is not. Supposing that my biggest fault were selfishness. I might go through the whole day without committing a sin—and yet the fault of selfishness would still be there, ready to spring into action upon provocation. A fault is a *root* of sin, a root from which sin will grow. If you have ever done any gardening, you know that you don't weed a garden just by cutting the weeds down; you don't get rid of the weed until you pull up the *root* of the weed.

Similarly, if we really are going to live Christ-like lives, it isn't enough to count up our sins and to say,

"O my God, I am sorry!" We have to get at the roots
of the sins. Consider the sin of anger, for example. If I
consciously give way to anger, I commit a sin. But the
question is, *why* do I get angry so easily? What is the
fault in me that leads to anger? Three different men
might get angry for three different reasons. With one
man it may be pride; he is so much in love with himself
that he thinks he is next to God Almighty; no one dares
to do anything to cross him. With another man, anger
might be due to laziness; he can't stand to have his comfort or his convenience interfered with. Still another
man might be angry because of his stubbornness, his
self-will; no one is going to push *him* around, no one is
going to tell *him* what to do.

We all have a good share of faults, the best of us. If
we try to overcome them, all at one time, we are likely
to end up by not getting rid of any of them; we shall
have spread our determination and our energy too thin.
I still can remember from childhood a story that was in
our fourth-grade reader. A parent was demonstrating to
his sons the strength of unity, the need for sticking
together. He took a bundle of small sticks and had each
son in turn try to break the bundle across his knee. Each
one failed to do so. Then the father untied the bundle
and showed them how easy it was to break the sticks,
one at a time. Applying that same fable in reverse, we
can see the need for attacking our faults one at a time.

We start with the biggest one, of course; always there
is some one *biggest* fault which each of us has: whether
it is pride or sensuality or lack of faith or covetousness—
or a subdivision of one of the greater faults, such as
obstinacy or selfishness or irreverence or stinginess. After
we get the biggest one licked, then we go on to the next

biggest one, and the next one, and so on down the line. It may take us a month or a year to conquer just one fault. We shan't worry about that, so long as we are making progress. The whole thing is a lifetime job, anyway.

Day by day we shall steadily become more Christ-like, but there will never come a time when we can sit back and say, "Now I am perfect; there is nothing more to be done!" We know that if ever we got to thinking that we were close to perfect, it would be a bad day for us. It would mean that we had become spiritually blind. We know that even if we live to be a hundred, we'll never be able to say that the task is finished, to say, "I am as perfect now as a man can be; there is no way in which I can improve myself." But that will not discourage us; because we know that God is satisfied so long as He sees us *trying;* He himself will finish off the work in Heaven.

As for the method, the technique of making our Particular Examen, there is no magic formula. We all are familiar with the essential steps, but it may be useful to review them. First of all I think it is well to start out with a word of thanks to God for His graces of the present day. We never do know all the graces which God gives to us each day: graces that He gives us in moments of temptation; temptations that He removes from our path because they might be too big for us; movements of grace within us that we don't recognize as such because they seem like good ideas of our own. No, we shan't know until Judgment Day all the countless graces that God has given to us every day. We never do say enough prayers of thanksgiving; starting our Examen with a word of gratitude will afford us another opportunity—and will put us in a good frame of mind to have true sorrow for not having used better the graces of today.

After our little prayer of thanksgiving, our next step is a quick appeal to the Holy Spirit, asking His help that we may have the light to see our faults and *the honesty to admit them*. It is not easy to be honest with ourselves. It is one of the hardest things in the world to see ourselves as we really are, to see ourselves as God sees us. In fact, it is hard even to see ourselves as other people see us, not to mention God. We would be surprised and maybe shocked if we knew what our own friends (I won't even mention enemies) really think of us. We build ourselves up so, in our own eyes; so often imagine ourselves much better (as we imagine ourselves much handsomer) than we really are. It is hard to look at ourselves squarely and without trying to put on a false front, even to ourselves.

We might, for example, set out to examine our conscience and be completely blind to the thing that needs working on the most. We have some definite fault, perhaps, which everyone else can see, but we won't even admit to ourselves that we have such a fault. You know how it can go: "I'm not stubborn; I'm just firm in adhering to principle." "I'm not selfish; I just don't believe in spoiling people." "I'm not stingy; I just happen to know the value of a dollar." "I'm not uncharitable; I just happen to believe that truth is truth." We all can add to that litany from our own experience.

Another danger is that, even if we admit that we do have a certain fault, it may be so dear to us that we try to evade its seriousness. We try to convince ourselves that some other fault is really bigger and should be worked on first. Perhaps our biggest fault is immortification, a pampering of self. We squirm at the thought of doing anything about it—so we decide to work on "distraction in prayer." Yes indeed, we do need the help of the Holy Spirit to have the honesty we must have, the *courage* we must have, to take a good square look at ourselves.

Then, having said our word of thanksgiving and our invocation of the Holy Ghost, we are ready to get down to business. When returning to the practice of Particular Examen after having neglected it for some time, or when determining on which fault to attack next, I think it is helpful to put Christ in our place. Imagine that He has lived through the same day which we have just finished (if this is in the evening); imagine that He literally was in our shoes, wearing our clothes, doing the same work we did, talking to the same people. As we follow along behind Him, we are very likely to come (maybe quickly) to a point where He and we part company; a spot in the day where He would have acted quite differently, spoken quite differently, than did we. The sharp word we spoke to the slow-moving assistant; the grumbling we did when the pastor asked us to do something; our evident annoyance when the school Superior made her request.

By the time we have followed Our Lord through one or two of our days, we should have a good idea of what our main fault is. And let's remember that it is the *root* we want to dig for; not just the weed on the surface. We don't say, "My main fault is anger"; but rather, "Now *why* do I get angry so easily?" Maybe it is selfishness. Maybe I am so self-centered that I won't go out of my way to be nice to anyone except my own particular friends. It never occurs to me to try to help others to enjoy themselves or to be happy. I am too wrapped up in myself.

Once we have established what our predominant fault is, then our Examen is concentrated on that fault daily until we have it under control, until we have developed the opposite virtue in its place. It might be worth noting in passing that our predominant fault isn't necessarily the one that manifests itself most often. It may be that my predominant fault is pride, let us say. A day might pass, or two or three, without my pride having occasion to assert itself. Meanwhile I have been unguarded with my eyes three or four times. This doesn't mean that I should immediately leave pride and switch to sensuality. It is the fault that is the deepest, the fault that is the dearest to me, the fault that is doing me the most spiritual harm, that I must keep working on. Or let us say, the fault which more than any other constitutes the greatest barrier between me and God.

During this part of our Examen—what we might call the heart and the essence of our Examen, as we look back through the past twenty-four hours to appraise our progress—let's remember again that it isn't just the elimination of a fault, but rather the implanting of a virtue, that is our principal aim. Consequently we do not look back merely to see where we may have surrendered to our weakness—we also take note of the occasions on which we have practiced the opposite virtue—and the missed opportunities when we *could* have practiced it, and didn't. It is a survey of the day, and it leads quite naturally to an act of sorrow for our failures. We know that God's grace has not been wanting, we know that we could have tried harder, we do want to be more generous with God—and we tell Him so.

After our look backwards, and a pause for a quick lifting of a repentant heart to God, we now swing our eyes forward to tomorrow and make our purpose of amendment. This probably is the most important part of our Particular Examen: our resolution for tomorrow. We might say that it is the *fruit* of our examen. We know that when a fruit tree, an apple tree let us say, grows up, it spreads out its branches and makes a nice shade. But the tree is of no real use unless it bears fruit. People do not plant fruit trees for the shade they can give, but for the fruit they will bear. Similarly we can say that if we make an examination of conscience (however carefully we do it) and nothing comes of it—then what is the good of it?

So now we look ahead to tomorrow. Suppose that the thing I am working on is my self-love. The virtue I am trying to acquire is thoughtfulness for others. Today I failed rather badly. I growled at the assistant because he carried the newspaper to his room before I had the crossword puzzle finished; I was sarcastic to the cook because the gravy was too greasy; I was snappish to that woman who telephoned during lunch time. I resolve that I shall be more on my guard tomorrow. I am going to take a positive joy in watching for chances to be pleasant, I shall go out of my way to say a word of praise, to do something thoughtful. I am going to be so cheerful and easy to get along with that everyone will think it is a dream, that it can't be true. I'm going to give the housekeeper and the assistant and the janitor and the nuns the surprise of their lives!

D

That's the way it works; very definite and specific plans for the day ahead. But we know that we shall never keep such resolutions without a lot of help from God, so we end our Particular Examen with a brief prayer asking God to give us the grace we shall need to persevere in our brave intentions. Our Particular Examen is finished.

It has taken much longer to talk about the Particular Examen than it will take to do it. Two or three minutes will be enough. Everything about it can be brief. A short prayer of thanksgiving: "Thanks, dear God, for the graces You gave me today, which I have used so poorly." A short prayer to the Holy Ghost: "Most Holy Spirit, help me to be perfectly honest with myself in making this examination." Then a quick backtracking on our day, with Jesus Himself leading the way; seeing very easily where we fell down on the resolutions we made yesterday. Next a short act of contrition: "Beloved God, I am truly sorry for my failures today, and for all the sins of my life; I promise You I *will* do better tomorrow." Then a quick look ahead, dropping a few mental markers on the danger spots, not expecting to change our whole life in a day but determining to change *right here* where we are putting our finger. Then finally the short but earnest appeal to God to help us keep our good intentions: "Blessed God, I am so craven and so weak, I can do nothing without You; please help me to follow through!"

Two or three minutes will do it all, if we do it every day. The time when we do it may vary with each of us. We may follow the seminary custom and make it a pre-dinner practice. Others may find it more practicable as a part of their night prayers. Still others may prefer to include it in their visit to the Blessed Sacrament. The important thing is to *do* it, and to persevere in it; to be smarter than the devil, who will try every ruse he knows to talk us out of it, to get us to abandon the practice. If we do persevere, we shall grow a little better each day, a little closer to the image of Christ, a little stronger in our love for Him. We shan't realize ourselves how much better we are becoming—and it's just as well that we do not. Other people will notice the change in us. God will notice the change in us. But we ourselves will never be satisfied (let us hope) that we are doing enough.

THE RESOLUTE PRIEST

"IF ANYONE say that a man once justified . . . is able, during his whole life, to avoid all sins, even those that are venial, except by a special grace from God, as the Church holds in regard to the Blessed Virgin; let him be anathema." Those are the words of the Council of Trent. The Tridentine Fathers were merely stating in more precise terms a decree of the fifth-century Second Council of Mileve, which stated that "Whoever holds that the words of the Our Father: 'Forgive us our trespasses,' when pronounced by saintly men, are pronounced in token of humility, but not truthfully, should be anathema."

Neither Council excepted priests from their pronouncements; so it is *de fide* that you and I are sinners: that we have sinned, and that we shall sin again. Neither Council, we know, is referring to mortal sin. The Council of Trent in another decree expressly states that "If any one say that the commandments of God are, even for one that is justified and constituted in grace, impossible to keep; let him be anathema."

In other words, there is no excuse for us, for any Christian, to commit mortal sin. But venial sin, at least semi-deliberate venial sin, is going to be an inescapable factor in our efforts to become better priests, to grow in love for God. We should be very foolish, then, if we tried to whistle our way past the dark cemetery; if we tried to pretend that sin was no problem in our priestly lives.

In facing the problem, mortal sin pre-eminently comes first in order of importance. It is, we know, a fully conscious, fully deliberate choice of our own will over God's Will, in a serious matter. It is a turning of our back upon God. It is a refusal to give God our love. We know that mortal sin does not necessarily destroy a priest's usefulness as a direct channel of God's grace. The bread and the wine will still become the Body and Blood, even though it be a priest in mortal sin who pronounces the words of consecration. The absolution he imparts will still wipe away the sins of others, even though the priest's own soul be in spiritual darkness. Even the words which he speaks, when it is God's truths which he utters, may persuade others to the practice of the very virtue which the preacher lacks.

No, in his primary role as a bearer of God's gifts to others, mortal sin will not wholly destroy the priest's usefulness. But in his secondary capacity, as the pattern of his flock, mortal sin certainly will diminish, perhaps to the vanishing point, the effectiveness of the priest. He cannot ignite the hearts of others with a flame which has been extinguished in his own heart. He will not have the quick instinct to discern spiritual needs, and the sure judgment in prescribing remedies for others, if both light and wisdom have disappeared from his own soul.

In appraising the danger of mortal sin in the life of a priest, probably most of us would designate lust as the one among the seven capital sins which constitutes the greatest threat. Because of our vow of perfect and absolute chastity, opposed to the counterthrusts of a rebellious passion which reason so imperfectly controls, we feel that it is here that our greatest danger lies. Whether or not it is our greatest peril, at least it is our most obvious one.

Probably, too, it is our most disturbing one. Because in matters that touch upon chastity, it is so difficult to be disinterested judges in our own case. The boundary between temptation and sin is such a narrow one, and knowledge-plus-consent is so seldom clearly defined, that even with the best will in the world we can easily be tormented by doubts and fears. We have to maintain the precarious balance between laxity on the one side (in which we push the principle of doubt to an unjustified extreme), and scrupulosity on the other side (in which we confuse purely physical manifestations of thoughtless and semi-voluntary actions with deliberate deeds).

Our dilemma would very readily be resolved, however, if we would try to view ourselves impersonally and judge ourselves as we would judge a penitent who was troubled by fears and uncertainties. "Listen," we might tell one penitent, "you are trying your best to lead a good life. You go to Confession every week; you are faithful to your morning and night prayers and your daily examination of conscience; you never miss daily Mass and Communion if you can help it; you never willingly put yourself in the occasion of sin; above all, you yourself admit that you don't *want* to sin—that the thought of sin, in your saner moments, horrifies you; you do try to remember to pray when you find yourself tempted; so *quit worrying*," we should tell such a penitent; "you're doing fine; your temptations are a cross that is gaining great merit for you in Heaven. Don't let the devil get you so worked up over this one thing that you haven't any energy left to work at some other virtues. Go in peace now, and God bless you!" Haven't we sometimes talked to others like that? Then why can't we talk that way to ourselves?

Of course we *couldn't* talk that way to ourselves if it wouldn't be true. There is another type of admonition sometimes needed. "Look now," we may have said to a penitent, "you're not really *trying* to do the right thing: You're very irregular about going to Confession; you admit that you neglect your prayers; your Masses and Communions are just routine; apparently you don't profit at all by past mistakes—you go right back to the same occasions of sin; you dabble with temptation as though it was something you could turn on and shut off at will; you don't even turn to God for help to overcome your own weakness; is it any wonder you're having trouble?"

Each must decide for himself which type of exhortation applies in his own case. With the great majority, and generally, I am sure that it will be the first one. It is well for us to have a wholesome fear of sin, but it would be a belittling of God if our vigilance were not liberally mixed with confidence. There may be cases where past habits are a complicating factor, calling for redoubled prayer and even heroic mortification. But certainly if we are trying day by day to be good priests, faithful to prayer, dedicated to the doing of God's Will —then certainly all doubts should be resolved in our favor. It will scarcely be credible that in a moment of weakness or of strong assault by passion, we shall reverse the whole tenor of our lives and deliberately abandon the Master we have been trying so hard to serve.

And let's not forget that there are other capital sins besides lust. It is true that purity is basic to priestliness; nothing will despiritualize a man more quickly than sins of the flesh. But it would be a great mistake to think that we are saintly priests simply because we are chaste priests. Sacerdotal holiness is not a one-virtue affair.

There is gluttony: another of the gross sins which can so coarsen and weaken the very fibre of a priest's spiritual being. I wish that our Blessed Mother would appear to some saint and command him or her to promote a total abstinence society among priests, at least in the whiskey-drinking countries. I am afraid that it would take our Blessed Mother herself to make the cause a popular one. Or maybe a magnetic crusader could do for priestly total abstinence what beloved Father Peyton has done for the Rosary.

The point is that most of us wouldn't miss liquor at all if we had the support of one another in its complete renunciation. Most of us will take a sociable drink or two with our priest friends or our family and will not even think of the stuff again until the next clerical gathering or family dinner. But there is that small percentage of us who just can't take that one or two drinks and stop there. There are those for whom alcohol is quick poison; for them it is either none—or curtains! Those of us whose appetites are normal can take no pride in the fact of our sobriety; and I am sure that the vast majority of us would gladly surrender our own mild use of intoxicants for the sake of our less fortunate brothers, if we could do it on a corporate basis.

Moving on to another root of sin which can play havoc with our strivings for virtue, there is the capital sin of anger. It is one of which very few of us can hold ourselves completely guiltless. With most of us it will be an occasional lapse and a brief lapse. But anger has become a major problem in the spiritual life of a priest if he has so lost control of his irascible appetite that he is habitually like a gas-filled oven—ready to blast at the slightest spark. He is a hard man to live with. He quarrels with his assistants, he scolds his people, he barks at callers who come to the rectory, he snaps at the housekeeper and reduces the nuns to tears. He is more of a scandal, on the whole, than the priest who drinks; he drives far more weak and wavering souls out of the Church.

And if his anger stems from pride, another of the capital sins, rather than from irascibility, then his state is even worse. If his fury is simply the fury of undisciplined anger, like the rage of a spoiled child, then he will have his good moments, when he will listen to reason and perhaps at times even admit that he may have been wrong. But if his anger is crossed with pride, then he cannot stand to be contradicted or opposed or questioned. In his self-blindness it will require a veritable miracle of grace to make him turn his eyes honestly inward, to see and acknowledge his own sinfulness. Even when he goes to Confession, he already is justified in his own eyes before ever the confessor speaks the absolving words.

Not all pride is an angry pride, however. There is a pride so deep that it disdains the weakness of anger. The priest who has succumbed to this type of pride faces the world with a chilly reserve. Sometimes he is given credit for great patience—because inwardly he is saying,

"I'm right and I know I'm right; why let myself get excited by the stupid fools I have to deal with?" He has no sense of humor of course; a sense of humor supposes the ability to laugh at oneself—and that he can never do. Generally he does but little harm to anyone but himself. His people may not love him, but they respect his manifest probity. He may make few converts and usually is not a popular confessor; but the people who leave his church *drift* away rather than are driven. He is a most unhappy man of course—the more so because he does not know it.

Then there is envy. So often it is hard, in our self-examination (and God forbid that we sin by judging anyone else!)—so often it is hard to distinguish between anger and pride and envy. Anger and pride fit so well together, and pride and envy are natural bedfellows. I really think a priest who never feels twinges of envy is far, far along the path to holiness. If we can listen to another priest being praised for a good sermon without a bit of inward writhing; if we can read of the promotion of a classmate and sincerely rejoice at his good fortune; if we can listen to one of our own parishioners telling us what a wonderful priest Father So-and-so is, without feeling a little cool towards that particular parishioner—well, we can skip the capital sin of envy in our examination of conscience. But if we find ourselves chronically critical of the accomplishments and the good fortune of others—particularly if deep-seated resentment of a brother priest has created enmity between us and him—then indeed do we have envy in its most virulent form. Then to us it is that Christ is speaking when he says, "If thou art offering thy gift at the altar, and there rememberest that thy brother has anything against thee, leave thy gift before the altar and go first to be reconciled to thy brother, and then come and offer thy gift."

Covetousness is another capital sin whose tentacles can reach into the life of the priest. Sometimes our covetousness is strictly personal. It manifests itself in a too great preoccupation with stole fees and stipends, too great a readiness to toss missionary literature into the wastebasket ("I've got a missionary parish myself") and to brush off other appeals to our charity ("If these people weren't so shiftless they wouldn't have to be asking for help"); always rationalizing; too quick to wonder (when asked, for example, to speak at some gathering), "How much will I get for it?", rather than, "How much good can I do?"; too concerned about our old-age security and the size of our bank account; too anxious to have the finest and best that money can buy, whether it be furniture or automobile or travel accommodations.

Then, besides being personally covetous, there is a covetousness that extends itself to our parochial administration. Money-talk then outrivals the Gospel as a pulpit topic. The poor begin to feel unwelcome in our church, and everyone begins to feel resentful; the anticlericals joyfully crow, "I told you so; all these priests care about is money." Meanwhile it hurts us every time money leaves the parish, it pains us to send a check to the chancery office, even if it is for the Holy Father or the Propagation of the Faith. Needless to say, no money of our own is included in the check.

And finally there is sloth. *Mea culpa, mea culpa, mea maxima culpa!* Can we say that we have never, as assistants, tried to dodge a bit of unpleasant or hard work, in the hope that someone else would get stuck with it instead? Can we say that we have never, as pastors, tried to fob a job off on an already overworked assistant, because the job would interfere with our own comfort and leisure? Let us not, pastors and assistants, point accusing fingers at each other here; let each of us turn his finger towards himself. How often the sick have gone unvisited, while we read or drowsed at home? How often sermons have gone unprepared, with loss to our people, while we have watched television or listened to the radio or to records or tinkered with a hobby? How often convert instructions have been hurried or curtailed to make way for a personal engagement of our own? How often has the solemn liturgy of the Church been massacred because we hadn't the ambition to review our ceremonies? Which of us has the temerity to talk about lazy pastors or lazy assistants, while he has a conscience of his own to examine?

These, then, are the seven capital sins: lust and gluttony, anger and pride and envy, covetousness and sloth. If we sin mortally, our sin will stem from one of these. But let us remember that we shall never sin through *mere* weakness or weariness; we shall never sin simply because in an unwary moment a trap was sprung at our feet. We shall not blind ourselves to the dangers, but neither shall we exaggerate the risk. "If anyone say that the commandments of God are . . . impossible to keep; let him be anathema." We are not saints, most of us, God knows. But, please God, we are men of good will. Honestly trying as we are, the present grace always will be equal to the present temptation. Among us happily there will be the noble exceptions—the men who stand out as the bright embodiment of all that a priest should be. But most of us are plodders, and will be plodders to the end. Our only claim to glory (it is a small one, so let us make the most of it)—our only claim to glory is that our successes will be more frequent than our failures, our forward steps always a little longer than our slippings-back. This, only, is asked of us: that we be determined, that we be persevering, that we be resolute. God's grace will do the rest.

THE GENEROUS PRIEST

When the Council of Trent pronounced anyone anathema who might maintain that a man could live his whole life through without a single sin, even venial, the Fathers erected a permanent barrier against the danger of spiritual pride. But how mistaken we should be if we concluded that, venial sin being inevitable, it suffices for us to try to avoid mortal sin.

Venial sin that is *fully deliberate* is avoidable, and we shall not be good priests unless we do labor to avoid it. A good priest, in fact a good man, is one who loves God with all his heart and soul. His love for God is a *supreme* love, placing God before everyone and everything else. How absurd it would be to make an Act of Love something like this: "O my God, I love Thee above all things with my whole heart and soul. I shall not let anything really *big* come between Thee and me—but of course, God, don't expect me to give up all the little self-attachments which are so dear to me."

We have only to put it in words to see how contradictory is such a state of mind. Yet it is exactly the state of mind of one who makes no effort, or but little effort, to avoid venial sin. Looking at it from a purely human viewpoint, it almost seems that the man who commits a mortal sin under the pressure of a powerful temptation is less culpable than he who measures out his love to God in selfishly calculated amounts. The habitual liar, for example, seems to us more contemptible than the out-and-out perjurer; the petty cheater more degraded than the absconding cashier.

In practice, of course, the two are seldom distinct from one another. We know that mortal sin is not a crashing disaster that suddenly hurtles into the life of a good man. Mortal sin is rather the spine-shaking thump at the bottom of the toboggan slide, the rending smash of a pilot who has stunted once too often. We know that no number of venial sins can add up to a mortal sin; but they surely can prepare the way. The man who has not learned to say "No" to himself in little things will not find it easy to say "No" when really vital interests are at stake.

My own understanding of Judas is that of a man who committed only one mortal sin. When Jesus chose him for an apostle, Judas must have had a very attractive soul. He was a young man, disingenuous in nature, devoted to his family, conscientious in his work, sincere in the practice of his Hebrew faith. We must remember that he, like the others, made an heroic act of self-renunciation; he too "left all things" to follow Christ. It probably wasn't much that he left—a battered boat and a tattered net—but it was a lot to Judas.

And then he was made the bursar for the apostolic band. He carried the purse in which they pooled their pennies and placed all donations; from it Judas paid the bills. He had never had much dealing with money before. His father sold the fish they caught; Judas was provided with his food and clothing and his other simple needs. But now he has money, real hard money. I can see Judas playing catch with the purse as he walks along, throwing it up in the air and loving the clink of the coins as it lands back in his fist. I can see him dumping the contents out in his palm and rubbing the silver between his hands. Just one little copper he finally takes for himself —just for a sort of souvenir. Next time perhaps two coppers, or a bit of silver; but never anything big. Judas doesn't have big ideas. Buying himself a bit of fried fish or a seed-cake in the market is excitement enough for him. But every little sin makes him a little weaker and a little blinder. He still loves God, within limits. He still is loyal to Jesus—although he is beginning to have doubts about that Kingdom that the Master has been promising to establish.

Then his big chance suddenly comes. The Sanhedrin will pay him thirty pieces of silver if he will lead them to Jesus. A *wonderful* opportunity! There can't be anything really wrong about it; he will get his money in advance, Jesus will escape from his captors as He always has done before. And the Sanhedrin deserve to lose their dirty money; maybe it will teach them a lesson. It all seems so plausible, so reasonable—as mortal sin always does, until after the sin is committed. With Judas, it was repeated venial sins which had dulled his perceptions and made it so easy for him to rationalize evil. It was repeated venial sins which laid the groundwork for his one big and doubly deadly sin. And it could happen to us.

So we try, as good priests must, to make our Act of Love ring true; we try to keep our service of God free from all compromise; we try to avoid all venial sin.

What are some of the venial sins that can intrude

themselves into the life of a priest? One of them, not widespread perhaps, but rather blood-chilling when we encounter it, is the sin of profanity; or perhaps I should say the habit of profanity. Moralists tell us that in the case of such a habit, it is not the individual lapses that are sinful; but that we sin each time we advert to the habit and fail to take any steps to break it.

I said that profanity in a priest, the irreverent use of the name of God and of Jesus Christ, is a blood-chilling thing even for another priest to listen to; we can imagine the effect it must have upon the layman. And make no mistake about it, a habit such as this cannot be tied up and turned loose at will, according to the company we are in. If we curse and use profanity in the company of other priests, the same words will escape us in other company too; and what was a venial sin of irreverence may easily become a mortal sin of scandal.

The malice of the sin lies in the very evident lack of love for God that is involved. We do not lightly bandy the names of those whom we love. A name is only a word, only a grouping of letters of the alphabet. But the name is so intimately related to him who bears it, that the mere mention of a name can arouse in us feelings of happiness or feelings of distaste, according to the associations the name has for us. Men have committed murder to vindicate the honor of a name; men have committed suicide because a name has been besmirched.

Certainly we are not living our day in the presence of God, if in every moment of impatience, annoyance or excitement, we use His Name as an expletive, or to give emphasis to what we say. I should not dare to judge an individual case, but I would say that in general a priest who has the habit of profanity, and is making no effort to break the habit, is in a serious state of tepidity and desperately needs to rededicate himself to the doing of God's Will, needs most urgently to pray for an increase in his waning love for Christ.

Another venial sin of speech to which we are exposed is the off-color story; and its ally, the double-meaning remark. We are all well-versed in the moral principle involved. We know that we may listen to and laugh at a so-called off-color story which really is funny and not patently obscene—provided we take no venereal pleasure in the story. We may even, without sin, tell such a story in a group of our own, when we are sure that no scandal will be given.

But who can judge with certainty where humor leaves off and obscenity begins? Who can be sure that no scandal has been given or taken? Have you never been present in a group when someone started off with a merely vulgar story, then someone chimed in with a double-meaning story, then someone capped that with a slightly smutty story, and the chain-reaction went on in a progressively downward course? No, we have only one choice as good priests—to keep our speech clean and chaste, as we try to keep our lives clean and chaste. When we are tempted to make ourselves the center of attention in a group by telling a story that is really funny but just a bit rancid—let us in that moment recall that we have offered to God "all that we do, think or say this day"; and ask ourselves whether God will consider this an acceptable part of our gift.

Then there is uncharitable speech (my, in how many ways our tongue can betray us!). I do not mean speech that is slanderous or calumnious; such talk is too often gravely sinful to deserve to be included here with the common venial sins. By uncharitable speech I mean the barbed criticisms that are so often directed against our absent brethren; the hashing over of their real or supposed faults; the imputing to them of unworthy motives; the belittling of their accomplishments; the grousing and the growling about the decisions of superiors; that whole area of clerical conversation that can only be classified as mud-raking.

It is in this especially that we must watch ourselves most closely. All of us have our inner resentments which seek outlet against someone, against anyone who will provide a convenient target. All of us have our deep-seated feelings of inferiority which seek bolstering at the expense of others. All of us have our private uncertainties which seek reassurance: reassurance that we must be pretty good, because see how bad these others are!

"Where two or three are gathered together for my sake, there I am in the midst of them," says Our Lord. Because Jesus so especially loves His priests, I am sure that He is especially among us, even when we are gathered together for relaxation and companionship. But surely He cannot stay long among us if we begin to use our tongues to reopen His wounds. And a clerical get-together can be lots of fun without having to resort either to shady stories or to malicious gossip. Any number of times I have been with a group of priests (and so have you) where the conversation would flow back and forth between a discussion of mutual problems, plans for the future, diocesan "dope," current events, sports— all of it interlarded with a generous amount of friendly ribbing—and everyone had a wonderful time, and no one went home with anything added to his examination of conscience.

There is another failure in speech which, while not common, is frequent enough. It is not always recognized as a matter of conscience, but it often is. This is the habit of sarcasm. It can be a matter of conscience because sarcasm rarely fails to wound the person against whom it is directed. If we deliberately hurt another unnecessarily, we have sinned against charity. Like individual instances of profanity, individual acts of sarcasm generally are not sinful, because the sarcastic speaker generally does not advert to the penetrating sharpness of his remarks. There is this about the habit, too, which makes it much more insidious than the habit of profanity: the latter is so manifestly wrong that the victim of the habit is much more likely to try to correct his profanity. The sarcastic person, on the other hand, is usually himself an insensitive sort, and finds it hard to recognize the evil of his speech. "Why," he will say, if a biting remark is called to his attention, "Why I didn't mean it that way at all; I was only kidding; can't the guy take a joke?" There may be exceptional occasions when mild sarcasm will have a place—but rarely when it is directed against an individual, present or absent. We shall sin far less by omitting sarcasm entirely than by trying to use it wisely. It is a tricky and a dangerous tool.

And now, how is our patience? I am not referring to lack of control over the passion of anger, but to that milder form of irascibility which frets and fumes inwardly and ofttimes outwardly—and sometimes snaps at others. It may be the hot weather or the cold coffee, the late newsboy or the stupid altar boy, the blown-out tire or the tardy convert. We do believe, don't we, that the doing of God's Will is the greatest of all goods, both absolutely and with regard to ourselves? We do believe that our greatest happiness, not just in Heaven but here and now, will result from the whole-hearted embracing of God's Will? We do believe that everything that happens to us, even the things that seem purely accidental, even the things that result from the malice or stupidity of others—are all part of God's plan for us, however obscure their purpose may seem? Then why, in the name of consistency, do we stew and simmer every time God's plan seems to run, even a little bit, counter to our own? But we do. Sadly I admit it from my own experience. We do.

The degree to which we inwardly squirm and outwardly complain at the happenstances of life is a good measure of the degree of interior recollection which we preserve through our day—a good measure of the extent to which we live our day in the presence of God. We shan't become more patient merely by resolving to do so. We shall become more patient only as we more and more supernaturalize our lives, through prayer and especially through meditation. Only so shall we develop that habitual consciousness that God is at work in every part of our day—and that the only thing that matters is that everything should work out the way He wants it to, no matter how confusing or even frustrating His ways may seem to us. This spirit of inner recollection, this underlying consciousness of God, even when we aren't actually thinking of God is something that any one of us can progressively develop by prayer and meditation. We come to the point, eventually, where our life is lived against God's Will as a backdrop. Impatience then will be a rare thing in our lives.

Another defect in priestly living, indeed in *Christian* living, is that of insincerity. I call it a defect rather than a sin, because really it is a character aberration that generally is a complexus of several faults. There may be a bit of pride involved, a bit of laziness, a bit of ambition, a bit of covetousness, a love of our own comfort: well, a lot of odds and ends that add up to selfishness.

Insincerity is a much easier thing to recognize than to define. An obvious (and, God be thanked, not too common) evidence of insincerity in a priest would be a tendency to play up to people of wealth and influence. It is very easy to be "broad-minded" and to make allowances for someone who has money, or is socially or politically prominent. It is equally easy to be very firm and strict with someone who is obscure and defenceless. We remember that one of the charges leveled against Christ by His enemies was that He spent too much time with publicans and sinners—with the poor and the outcast. If we hope to be truly Christ-like, we must try to deserve to have the same accusation directed against ourselves.

The insincere man (priest or otherwise) likes to use people. He will make a great fuss over someone from whom he is trying to get something, or over someone who he thinks may be useful to him; but he is ready to brush such people off very quickly if they begin to make any demands upon his own generosity. He likes to manoeuvre people, too, does the insincere man. He will use all sorts of devious stratagems to bring about what he wants—so that it may seem to have come without any seeking of his own. If he does do a deed that could be classified as charity, he manages to see that his bigheartedness is accidentally discovered. He is a man who never sticks his neck out, a man who rarely says "Yea, yea" or "Nay, nay"; he hesitates to take a strong position on anything, even a matter of principle, until he has found which way the wind is blowing. He never offers outright opposition when something is proposed that he doesn't like—not if duplicity will do instead. "Yes, yes, that's a splendid idea," he will say, and then proceed quietly to sabotage, even while he preserves an attitude of sad regret at the failure.

He is a hand-shaker, an opportunist, a politician (states-men, please forgive the simile) a double-dealer. We all have met him at one time or another; we even may have caught glimpses of him in our own mirror. Because absolute sincerity is not easy to achieve. If we watch closely enough, most of us can catch ourselves now and then in petty deceits and ignoble frauds of one kind or another. We can count it a grace if we do catch ourselves in such moments of guile, if we do feel stirrings of shame that we have failed to keep our vision clear and our purpose single. The pitiable man is the man who has so perfected himself in deceit that he even can deceive himself; the man who has achieved the feat of never letting his head know what his heart is doing.

Complete personal integrity is something for all of us to aim at. It is a lovable quality in any man; it is especially essential to the priest. We know that from our own experience. Those of our fellow-priests who possess this absolute probity of character—how plainly we can see the good that they do. We ourselves love them and admire them; they are the men we prize as confessors, advisers, spiritual directors.

And the whole secret of their openness, their un-affected and consistent honesty, lies in their generosity with God. Again and again I find myself coming back to that point in my own meditations. Whatever the subject of the meditation may be, whatever the virtue to be acquired or the vice to be suppressed, always in the end the conclusion is this: If I am really convinced that I am wholly God's, that all that I am and have belongs to God; that the only thing that matters is the accomplishment of His will in me, in the way He wants to accomplish it—then there will be a supernatural logic and soundness in all that I do. My time is God's, my talents are God's, my health is God's. I must make very sure that the fruit of them, the fruit of my labors, is God's fruit and not my own; even my failures must be God's.

Indeed, all that I have discussed here—the whole problem of venial sin and priestly imperfection—can be wrapped up in that one word, GENEROSITY; generosity with God; generosity with my money, my time, my comfort, my health—with my *self*. And in the final summing up, of course, it really doesn't deserve the name of generosity at all. It really is but the most basic form of justice that I should give back to God, without trying to save any for myself, the fullness of the riches that He has given to me.

THE REPENTANT PRIEST

IT WOULD seem a rather puerile sort of thing to do, to speak to priests about the Sacrament of Penance. We all have explained this sacrament so often to others—in sermons, in convert instructions, in catechism classes—that there surely is no corner of it that we have left unexplored. Yet in this, as in so many other points of our own spiritual lives, we need to have that salutary fear expressed by St. Paul: "Lest," as he says, "perhaps in preaching to others I myself should be rejected." We can and do often enough speak to our people of the Sacrament of Penance as a means of perfection; let us be sure that we ourselves do not disesteem it as an important factor in our spiritual growth.

We know that the primary purpose of this sacrament is to forgive mortal sin and to restore sanctifying grace to the soul that has lost it. Once we have been baptized, there is for us just no other way to have our mortal sins forgiven except through Confession. I am not forgetting that an act of perfect contrition—sorrow for sin based on love for God—will immediately forgive mortal sin. But we know that such an act of perfect contrition must include the intention to receive the Sacrament of Penance as soon as possible, if I am going to continue offering Mass. If I commit a mortal sin, the sin is forgiven the moment I make an act of perfect contrition; but if I then neglect to go to Confession even when I have the opportunity of doing so, I become guilty of a new mortal sin; because I violate the divine precept which demands that all post-baptismal sins be confessed before receiving Holy Communion. That is why we say that in practice there is no forgiveness for mortal sin except through the Sacrament of Penance.

We all are well enough acquainted with the deadly effects of grievous sin, not to neglect the Sacrament of Penance if we have need of it. In the life of a priest, especially, mortal sin is *such* a catastrophe. Because of his pastoral office he must celebrate Mass, he must dispense the sacraments—and as he unholily handles holy things, mortal sin after mortal sin is piled up to his account. Then there is the complete cessation of all supernatural life within him. The whole wonderful thing that happened to him in Baptism is now undone.

Before Baptism he had only a natural life—even his immortality was a natural immortality. As he grew older, he would be able to think and talk and walk and love; but everything he did would be on a merely natural level. He would be like a man shut up in a room with a ceiling overhead; a man who could throw a ball just so high, just so far and no farther. But he was baptized— and a change took place that would be incredible but for the credence of Faith. The ceiling and roof were snatched away, the walls fell to the ground. The Holy Ghost, eternally proceeding on His mission of love between God the Father and God the Son dipped quickly down, as it were, and caught this soul up into His eternal flow. The soul was transformed, with a brightness and beauty that is the reflected brilliance of God Himself. But it was not only the appearance that changed; the soul now pulsated with a vitality that was a sharing of God's own Life. It was not merely an increasing of strength and an extension of power; it was a whole new kind of life that the soul now began to live—a new kind of life in which the mere drawing of a breath could reverberate through the heavens and have an eternal value.

Then he committed a mortal sin, let us suppose. With a violent twist he hurtled himself out of the stream of Love and plummetted back into the darkness again; a lonely darkness, in which the sinner stands a solitary figure, cut off from God and from angels and from saints; cut off, effectively if not actually, from his fellow-members in Christ's Mystical Body—so that the ceaseless interchange of prayers and merits and graces flows around him and over him as though he were not there.

And not a thing that he does has any value now, or meaning, or any merit for himself. A moment ago he could have stooped to tie his shoe-lace, and all Heaven would rejoice. Now he can preach with such power as to make men weep; he can raise aloft the Host and Chalice for others to adore; he can comfort the sorrowing mother and convert the obdurate sinner and empty his wallet for the poor—and not a bit of it counts for him. So far as he is concerned, none of it is any more substantial than something he might have dreamed just before shutting off the alarm clock. Not a bit of it counts for him until he has cried out, "God have mercy!"

It is a terrible thing to commit a mortal sin, to reject God's love and to abandon the life we share with Him. It is an even more terrible thing to remain in the state of mortal sin, perhaps for hours, for days, for weeks. If only the clock could have a voice, and could whisper to the sinner with each moment that it ticks away, "Lost, lost, lost, lost"!

What a pitiable figure a priest would be who had surrendered himself to living for long periods, perhaps habitually, in the state of mortal sin. Day after day he would frustrate grace. Day after day the roots of sin would sink deeper. Day after day his faith would grow weaker. Day after day his hope in God's mercy would further droop and fade.

Notice that I say *his* hope in God's mercy. God's mercy itself would never diminish; until the end, Christ's love would never give up. There is no overestimating Our Lord's compassion for the sinner, be the sinner priest or layman; but *especially* when it is one of His priests, one whom He has chosen for His own, must Our Lord have a yearning eagerness to see the sinner turn back to Him. Particularly when the sin has begun perhaps in weakness, and the sinner has floundered more in confusion than in malice, as he has entangled himself more and more in the net of his own disordered will. We think of Peter, for whose sin there was seemingly so little excuse: he was a witness to the Transfiguration, he had been promised the primacy in Christ's Church, he had received so many graces from the Master. And his faith was strong ("Thou art the Christ, the Son of the living God," he had said); and his love for Christ was real ("Lord, to whom shall we go? Thou hast the words of eternal life!"). He had courage too; Peter was the only one to raise a hand to defend Jesus in the Garden of Olives, and he did follow Jesus to the High Priest's courtyard. Yes, Peter had abundant graces, and he had faith and love and courage to boot (dare any of us feel too sure of ourselves?); so in a sense his sin was the less excusable.

Yet how quickly Our Lord forgave Peter, once the apostle took his eyes off the phantoms in the fire and turned his eyes again towards Christ! And how kindly and how gently He gave Peter opportunity for reparation; no scolding, no harshness; just a softly spoken question, three times repeated: "Simon Peter, lovest thou Me? Simon Peter, lovest thou Me? Simon Peter, lovest thou Me more than these?"

And the doubting Thomas, too; again, so inexcusable in his incredulity. After three years in close company with Our Lord, after hearing all the prophecies of His resurrection; and then not willing even to believe the eye-witnesses who had seen the Lord. But his sorrow when it came was complete; there was no mistaking the agony in his act of contrition: "My Lord and my God!" There was no mistaking either the completeness of his forgiveness, as Jesus ended the whole matter with His simple admonition, "Be not incredulous, but believing."

There is no excuse, ever, for any of us to commit mortal sin. The very fact that sin is so inexcusable, especially in one who has been favored by Christ and is close to Christ, should give us some inkling of what the infinite mercy of God means—so quick and so willing to wipe clean and take back again the soul, no matter how deeply encrusted with sin—at the very first sign of repentance. And not just once, let us remember. God is not less merciful than His own creatures—and He charged His disciples that they must be ready to forgive "seventy times seven"!

"Come back, come back, come back" is Christ's never-silenced plea to His erring ones. From Peter and from Thomas the priest who has sinned takes courage. Yet he must know that if in his sin he delays too long, there may come for him, as there came for Judas, the point of no return. God's love and mercy will not die, but our own trust in His mercy can die; we can forget what it means to make a real act of contrition, as Judas did.

So the primary purpose of the Sacrament of Penance is to forgive mortal sin and to restore sanctifying grace to the soul. But in Confession Christ is not waiting merely to welcome us back; He is waiting there also to speed us on. For those who have used well their graces and have kept from serious sin, the Sacrament of Penance is a potent aid towards the progressive purification of our lives. The special sacramental grace of this sacrament is that it builds up in us a *resistance* to sin, a toughening against temptation. If we go to Confession regularly and frequently, then we know that when temptation comes there will be not merely adequate grace but abundant grace to meet the temptation. Not only shall we be quick to reject the enticement to grave sin, but venial sins too will become more and more easy to eradicate. We have preached this so often to others—and yet sometimes we can be so lax ourselves.

It can be difficult at times to get to Confession. We may be very busy. The priest to whom we usually go to Confession may live at a distance. We haven't done anything very serious since our last Confession, so it can wait another week—and another week and another week. The devil, of course, will be very diligent in helping us to find excuses; it makes things easier for him. Each time that we put off our Confession, graces are lost to us that we may need badly, we never know when.

Our first resolution, then, with regard to Confession—our first resolution as men who are striving for the whole-souled giving of ourselves to God—will be to receive the Sacrament of Penance every week if it is at all possible. And if it does happen that we have to miss one week, we shall not make that the first in a whole series of misses.

Our second resolution will be to make a *good* Confession; to get from the sacrament all the grace that we can. We know that only two things are required of us for a good and fruitful Confession: the telling of our certainly mortal sins, and genuine sorrow for our sins. Doubtful sins need not be confessed. Even if the matter was manifestly grave, yet if there is honest uncertainty in our mind as to whether we fully realized what we were doing, or whether there was full consent—then the sin need not be confessed. However, I think that we will agree that it is far better to mention such sins, as God may see us guilty; it may save us from painful scruples and worrisome uncertainty later on.

Normally it will be venial sins that will provide the matter for our Confession. One difficulty here may be that we cannot *remember* any sins, even venial, since our last Confession. If that happens very frequently, perhaps it points to too hasty an examination of conscience—or even to an outright neglect of an examination of conscience. We should never let ourselves develop the habit of "routine" confessions: popping in on our confessor on our regular day and running through the same unvarying monologue that we gave him last week and the week before: "Bless me father I have sinned I was uncharitable I was impatient I was distracted at prayer I was slothful in my work for these and for all the sins of my past life . . ."; proceeding on the assumption that we probably did some of these things and we might as well give ourselves full coverage. Confession is a *sacrament*, too sacred and serious an action to fulfill lightly and carelessly.

We need to make an adequate examination of conscience before our Confession, and come to it prayerfully and reverently, if it is to be the help to us that it can be in making us more Christ-like. Perhaps one cause of our difficulty in recalling possible sins at the time of Confession may lie in a neglect of the *daily* examination of conscience which should be a part of our evening prayers. Have you ever noticed how, when you awaken from a vivid dream, all the details of the dream are clearly present in your mind? By the time you have washed and shaved the details of the dream already have grown hazy. By the time you've had breakfast you have forgotten all about the dream.

Sometimes it is like that with our venial sins. At the moment of our failure we are conscious that we have done wrong—whether it was a rash judgment passed, a momentary impatience, or whatever. But the memory quickly fades unless such sins are fixed in mind by a daily scrutiny. If we examine our conscience only once a week at the time of our Confession, we remember practically nothing—and yet we have the realization that we just aren't as good as that. Meanwhile, because we aren't getting a true picture of ourselves, our progress, our improvement, will be slow.

Of course there may be weeks when there really haven't been any sins at all—nothing in the least deliberate, that is. If we really are trying hard to be good priests, to do God's Will, and are making full use of the means of grace—then there *should* be weeks like that once in a while surely. When the Fathers of Trent said that no man could go all his life without committing venial sin, they didn't mean that he couldn't go for one day or one week. In the years that are past we probably have done far more than enough to qualify under the Tridentine decree.

Besides the honest telling of our mortal sins, there is only one other thing required of us for the fruitful reception of the Sacrament of Penance: that is, true sorrow for our sins. In this, even more than in the telling of our sins, we have to guard against the debilitating force of routine. While sorrow that is even virtually present during Confession will suffice for validity, yet it is not merely a *valid* sacrament with a minimum of grace that we want to receive. Here for this moment the flood-gates of God's mercy will be wide open; it is more than a mere trickle of that mercy that we want to gain for ourselves.

Probably you in your own sermons have used that story of the long-time sinner who went finally to Confession. When he had finished his confession, the confessor imposed as a penance the Rosary, to be recited every day for a week. The penitent was aghast. "Father," he exclaimed, "surely I ought to have a bigger penance than that! I have betrayed God's love so often, I have offended Him so grievously, and He has been so patient with me!" "Well," answered the confessor, "if you feel that sorry, then maybe it would be enough to say *one* Rosary." The penitent broke down completely then; between sobs the confessor could hear him say, "God

E

has been so good, and I have been so bad!" "All right, then," said the confessor, "if that is how you feel, just say five Our Fathers and five Hail Marys." If it is advisable (and it is) to remind our people from time to time that the greater their sorrow, the greater will be their grace—it is well to remind ourselves of the same thing.

We know that genuine sorrow must include a genuine purpose of amendment—an earnest act of the will in which we pledge God that we shall not disobey Him again. For validity, it is enough that our purpose of amendment extend to all mortal sin. But, here again, the maximum of grace is what we want. We are not tepid souls, trying to buy Heaven at a bargain price. We are Christ's chosen ones, His very own. It will be not merely mortal sin, but *all deliberate sin* that we shall set our will against, as we make our act of contrition.

There is only one way to measure the firmness of our purpose of amendment. It will be measured by the degree with which we do seriously strive to avoid, in the future, the sins which we have confessed in the past. It would be worse than useless to go on confessing the same old sins time after time, if we were taking no serious steps to eliminate those sins from our lives. If it were a matter of venial sins which we were confessing, and which we made no sustained effort to avoid, we know that the sacrament still would be valid so long as our will was set against mortal sins. Yet there would be a grace-wasting indifference that would seem to border on hypocrisy.

If mortal sin *were* a problem, we should need to subject ourselves to a most searching self-study, if the same sin kept repeating itself again and again. Am I genuinely

easy virtue to practice. If a person loves God, he will want to do God's Will. If he always seeks to do God's Will, then he always will be doing the right thing. So it would seem to follow that Prudence is just another aspect of love for God.

But it is not quite as simple as that. A person who loves God and seeks only God's Will, normally will do the right thing *subjectively*. But what he sees as God's Will, what he deems to be the right thing, may be objectively the wrong thing. Such a man may be right in his conscience but wrong in his judgment, wrong in his deed.

The interdependence and interaction of one virtue upon another is so involved and so delicate that no one can hope to trace, with complete success, each thread in the fabric of any particular virtue. But it would seem to be very evident that humility must play a big part in the practice of Prudence. A man who has absolute confidence in the infallibility of his own judgments, who is certain that a thing is right because it seems right to him, will inevitably pull boners. Indecisiveness is a fault. A man who can't make up his mind never gets anything done. But it is not indecisiveness to stop and think twice before embarking upon a course of action that is in any way extraordinary—especially if it is an action that may have serious consequences. That is not indecisiveness, it is just good sense, it is Prudence.

Always supposing that we do love God and do seek His Will only (an indispensable foundation), the practice of Prudence requires above all the ability to put ourselves in the other fellow's place; in other words, the ability to stand off at a distance and look at ourselves objectively. If I contemplate some action that is in any way questionable as to its wisdom, I need to ask myself, "What would I say if some other priest were about to do this, and came to me for advice? Would I give it full approval or not?" Perhaps I will answer myself by saying, "Ah, but the same unique circumstances could not exist in the case of another priest; another priest could not carry this off like I can!" If that is the way I answer myself, then indeed is there need of pause; there is a strong smell of pride in the air.

Remembering St. Paul's warning that all things lawful are not expedient, Prudence will always dictate (before major or doubtful action) that we ask ourselves, "How will this look to people? Will the normal man of good will be able to see the rightness of it, the reasonableness of it? Are my motives, my reasons, my objectives quite clear; or is it something that will take a lot of explaining to allay mistrust and to quiet troubled consciences?" It is not an absolute rule, of course, but we may say in general that any action that requires a lot of explaining is more than likely an imprudent action. Prudence demands not only that we be right but that our rightness be evident to reasonable persons.

Perhaps it is time now that we got down to cases and examined Prudence at work in the everyday life of the priest. We might distinguish first of all between what could be called *personal* as distinguished from professional prudence: the prudence that guides us in our personal deportment and contacts, as distinguished from the prudence that guides us in our work. Personal prudence will cause us always to act in the way that a priest ought to act, in the way that our people have a right to expect us to act. In other words, a prudent priest will be first and foremost a *priestly* priest. He will always maintain that priestly reserve which is not a stand-offishness but which is a sense of reverence for his own priesthood, for the Christ he bears within him wherever he goes.

Personal prudence will reflect itself too in a priest's dress. Whether we realize it or not, our people feel vaguely uncomfortable with us when we are out of our regimentals. No one expects a priest to wear a Roman collar on the golf course or in the swimming pool. But certainly when we answer the door at the rectory, when we go shopping, when we travel about the parish on business or on pleasure bent—in fact, any time that the wearing of the collar would not be utterly ridiculous, we ought to have it on. The weather may be warm, but there should be *some* penance in our priestly lives. We might better have people say, "My, but Father looks hot in that black outfit" than to have them say, "My, you'd never know he was a priest, would you?" When we look back to the time we first put on a clerical collar, and remember how proud and thrilled we were to assume the sacerdotal dress, it does seem a pity that the passing years should have made it so chafing to our necks.

In our contacts with the womenfolk, too, personal prudence will guide us. Whether it be the housekeeper, the parish secretary, the Altar Society president, the lady converts, the young women in our school and parish: always the duty is upon us to keep them conscious of our priesthood. If familiarity enters, always we may be sure that it is we, not they, who first have let down the bars. And I scarcely need to repeat what has so often been said before: that it is not enough for us to have a good conscience; we must have a good reputation as well. I recall one good priest who caused a considerable amount of misunderstanding by the overly paternal interest he took in an orphan girl of adolescent age. The priest's motives were unimpeachable, but his methods were imprudent. Any time we find ourselves tempted to say, "Let them think what they want to; my own conscience is clear"; or say, perhaps, "I've got *some* rights as a man; this is still a free country even if I am a priest!" —any time we catch ourselves talking that way, it is more than likely that our prudence needs an overhauling.

Vacation is another good time to test our prudence. If we never seek recreations or amusements that we would be reluctant to indulge in at home; if we never go to places where a Roman collar would stand out like a contradiction; if our altar boys could see us at any time and not be scandalized—then prudence has gone with us on our holiday. Parenthetically I might remark that in my own efforts to practice prudence (and God forgive me all the times I've failed!) I find myself again and again casting back to my own boyhood and youth, to the high ideal of the priesthood that then was mine. I only have to be what I, as a boy, expected my own pastor and assistant to be—what in fact they were—and I shall do all right in the matter of prudence. As I write this a memory comes back to me from childhood. Another kid and I were standing in front of the hootchy-kootchie show at the County Fair, watching the girls wiggle their hips while the barker did his spiel. Our assistant pastor came strolling along the Midway, wearing his Roman collar of course. He spotted us and smiled and without breaking his stride said, "Let's go over and go through the fun house, shall we?" I was a bit ashamed, of course, but somehow proud, too; proud of being a Catholic and of having a priest like that. It's strange how that long-forgotten scene pops up in my mind now.

Well, I need to be prudent in my speech, too. Sometimes my sense of humor isn't as funny as I think it is. I need to be careful not to talk jokingly to someone who is trying to be serious, not to make light of what is a serious matter to him, not to make wisecracks that may give offense or be misunderstood. A sense of humor can be a dangerous thing if it is unleashed at the wrong time or with the wrong person. Prudence in speech also will keep me from lashing out at people with cutting or scathing remarks, from raising my voice at them and telling them off, regardless of the provocation they may seem to give me. This is particularly a danger when on the phone or writing a letter; it is so much easier to be nasty with someone you cannot see. Whether I see them or not, prudence will be the governor that keeps me always the priest and never the mere man.

But we had better get on to consider some of the applications of prudence in our parochial work, as distinguished from prudence in our personal conduct. One area in which pastoral prudence must be vigilant is in our preaching. It is so easy, especially if we are feeling irritable and below par, to use the pulpit as an outlet for our feelings. I don't suppose that any of us would ever be so lacking in prudence (not to mention charity) as to indulge in personalities in the pulpit, using it to criticize or condemn individuals. That, even if it is done without naming names but only by implication and innuendo, is one of the worst of pastoral sins. Yet it is imprudent, too, to pillory a whole class of people: to declaim upon the laxity of parents or the featherheadedness of young people or the hypocrisy of Protestants. There are parents listening to us, there are young people listening to us, there is a man in the front pew whose saintly mother was a staunch Methodist. Above all at funerals must we tread with care—and with kindness. The late lamented may have been out of church for years before his doubtful deathbed repentance, and perhaps it is the first time in years that many of the mourners have been in church. But they are there in grief now, and it is for us to comfort, not to flay. In all of our preaching we have to keep reminding ourselves that we do not change hearts by scolding, we do not make conversions with tirades. In the pulpit, as nowhere else, must prudence ride with a tight rein upon impatience or a temporarily soured disposition.

The whole field of administration is another part of our work which prudence can do much to make lighter. Take the matter of new construction. How many parishes there are which have been saddled with intolerable debt because the pastor, like the man in the Gospel, afford it?", but also asks, "Do we really need it?" Sometimes our desire for outstanding achievement can carry away our cool judgment and plunge us into a building failed to realistically assess his resources before undertaking to build. Prudence not only asks, "Can we really program whose usefulness is not commensurate with its cost. I know of one parish where the pastor built a beautiful big parish hall and recreation center because, he said, they needed a place to hold parties to raise money for the parish, and a social center for the young people. Well, all the money that has been raised since has gone to pay for the hall itself. And I am not sure that the good that has accrued to the young people is commensurate with the dissatisfaction of the parishioners who are being hounded so for money.

The Church by its nature is hierarchical, and there is

no place in its government for what we commonly term democracy. Yet there seems no good reason why the people of the parish should not be given some voice in the expenditure of their own money. Conceding that there are times when a pastor must proceed with a needed work even against the disapproval of many parishioners—perhaps the construction of a school—and conceding that the last word and the final responsibility must always rest with the Ordinary, it still seems feasible to take a vote of the parishioners, through questionnaires placed in the pews or sent through the mail, as to their wishes in regard to a contemplated major improvement, or with regard to a notable change in parish policy. Many successful parish administrators have tried this very thing and have discovered that people who have some small voice in the administration of their parish will in the end take a much greater interest in the physical as well as the spiritual welfare of their parish.

It is prudence too that will enable us to listen to the hesitant suggestions offered by parishioners, to the constructive criticism voiced by parish committeemen. Instead of fuming inwardly that anyone should presume to know more than we, instead of saying to ourselves (or worse, saying to someone else), "There's that stupid fool shooting off his mouth again," prudence will weigh well and objectively every counsel or recommendation proposed, without any pettiness of injured pride. We priests have so much God-given power in our hands as it is; there is by necessity so much that is autocratic in what we do; it will be a pity if we surrender to delusions of grandeur and place ourselves on a higher pedestal of omniscience than we have any right to.

Prudence plays such a vital role in so much of our

parochial work. It is prudence that will keep us from setting up impossible goals of behavior or achievement for our altar boys, our young people's club, or any other group with whom we have to deal. It is prudence that will preserve us from the folly of trying to make converts by attacks upon Protestants, rather than by a positive presentation of the Catholic position. It is prudence that will lead us to study thoroughly and prepare ourselves well for any new movement or organization we contemplate introducing into our parish. It is prudence that will make our ministry in the confessional a fruitful one. It is prudence that will protect us from involvement in local political disputes, from taking sides in family quarrels. It is prudence that will inspire us to let the trained educational personnel run the school, and will check any impulse we may have to interfere with something that is not our specialty.

There is no end to the fields in which prudence will function in the life and the work of the priest. It would be folly to try to list them all here, much less discuss them all. What has been said has not been said with any thought or intention of *teaching* anyone prudence. Prudence is acquired by habit and infused by God; it is not learned from a book or a lecture. My only purpose has been to share with others the self-examination which you and I, being human, have need to renew from time to time, on our possible failures in this virtue. The most imprudent man in the world, I think, would be the man who would feel superior to any need for increase in prudence. It is an increase that will come readily enough to the man of genuine good will who asks for it in prayer, with a prayer that rises humbly from the memory of and the admission of his own many imprudences.

There is no one who can better teach us prudence and more surely win the grace of it for us than she who, uniquely among us humans, so perfectly exemplified it both by nature and by grace. No better aspiration could rise frequently to our lips, especially in those moments when our own judgment is ringing its little warning bell, than "Virgin most prudent, pray for us!"

THE BROTHERLY PRIEST

To ME, one of the most beautiful passages in all the Bible is Christ's prayer after the Last Supper, for His disciples and for His Church. It is a prayer in which the Master pleads passionately, with all the intensity of which His Sacred Person is capable, for two things: love and unity.

We can read the passage over and over again, and find some new spark of thought at every reading. At the moment, I should like to dwell on the note of unity. Unity is the mark which Christ Himself points to as being the final and unanswerable proof of the divinity of His mission. We are called upon to be witnesses to Christ, men who will daily and irrefutably bear testimony to the fact that Jesus Christ is the Son of God. In the first chapter of the Acts, Jesus tells His disciples, "You shall receive power when the Holy Spirit comes upon you, and you shall be witnesses for Me in Jerusalem and in all Judea and Samaria and even to the very ends of the earth."

He was harking back, when He said that, to His Holy Thursday prayer. It was then that He pleaded: "Holy Father, keep in Thy name those whom Thou hast given

Me, that they may be one even as we are. . . . Yet not only for these do I pray, but for those also who through their word are to believe in Me, that all may be one, even as Thou, Father, in Me and I in Thee; that they also may be one in us, *that the world may believe that Thou hast sent Me.*"

If Christ's words mean anything, they mean that we who claim to be His followers must present a united front to the world; not the regimented unity of an army, not the accidental unity of nationality or race, but the unity of a family, the cohesive unity of love.

This is true of all believers—and doubly and triply true for priests. No matter how important our work may be, it all will be so much wasted effort so far as Our Lord is concerned, unless we are doing our full part to contribute to the unity of the Mystical Body of Christ. Even if I were the most eloquent preacher in the state, the best teacher on the campus, the smartest administrator in the diocese—it would mean nothing unless at the same time I were an unmistakable link in the unity for which Christ prayed.

To get down to hard facts, we might say that there are two directions in which our zeal for unity will especially show itself. First of all there will be our complete and unreserved unity with Christ in His Church. "*Sentire cum ecclesia*" always has been the mark of the true Christian; it must be burned deep into the heart of the priest.

There is no danger, I am sure, that any of us teeter on the brink of heresy or apostasy. But little things can be destructive of unity too; like the hairline cracks in masonry which ultimately may bring the entire wall to ruin. One straw in the wind by which we can test our own spirit of unity is our attitude towards the directives of Canon Law and the prescriptions of the rubrics. If our obedience to Canon Law in our priestly life and work, and our observance of the rubrics in our Mass and in the administration of the sacraments, is habitually a *minimal* obedience—then we are failing Christ. If our only anxiety is to discover whether a canon or a rubric binds "*sub poena peccati,*" and we dismiss everything else with an airy "Why worry?"—then ours is not Christ's idea of unity. He speaks through His Church on matters other than sin.

As we get closer home in meditating on this question of unity, there is need to consider our relations with our own Ordinary and his delegates in the various diocesan offices. What *is* our attitude towards diocesan official-dom? Do we view every episcopal letter with suspicion, every diocesan decree or statute with resentment—as a galling bond to be evaded if possible? I don't suppose that any bishop can be right a hundred per cent of the time—and the batting average might be even lower for chancellors and lesser officials. But they do see things from a much better vantage point than the individual priest, with a much wider horizon. And they are as conscious as you or I of the fact that they will one day answer to our common Master for their decisions and their deeds. But aside from that, the point is that you and I *will* be right a hundred per cent of the time if we give quick and cheerful acceptance to the Will of God as it comes to us through pope or bishop or vicar.

I do not mean that Christ intends us to abandon the use of the intelligence which He has given us. In matters that do not pertain to faith or morals, we have a right—at times an obligation—to express an opinion, to offer constructive criticism. And if we do so through proper channels, in an accompanying spirit of charity and obedience, there is no wound to unity. The Holy Father's restoration of the Easter Vigil service, his changes in the law of Eucharistic fast, his permission for evening Masses, the vernacular ritual now allowed in several countries—all were in response to representations from bishops and priests who felt the urgent need for such changes in today's world. But we may be sure that such requests were made in no spirit of insubordination or rebellion.

Besides the necessity of preserving unity of spirit between ourselves and Christ in His Church there is the fundamental obligation also of being at one with our brother priests. If we are going to be practical, this at once raises the question of the pastor-assistant relationship. I know that I incur the danger of wrath from both sides by touching upon the question, but I think that we all will agree that it is in the rectory, where men must live and work together twenty-four hours a day and seven days a week, that the fabric of unity is most often in danger of being torn; the unity which Jesus most especially prayed might characterize His disciples.

Perhaps it would be expecting a miracle that any two or three or four people should live in close confinement with one another, day after day, without occasionally getting in one another's hair. Our faults become so mercilessly exposed to the view of one another. And strangely enough it usually is the most petty faults of personality, rather than major faults of character, which become the greatest source of irritation. The way that one man slurps his soup or sniffles his nose or musses up the newspaper can set another man's teeth on edge.

It is worth remembering that pastor-assistant tensions are as old as the Christian Church. Paul and Barnabas had to split up, you will recall, because they just couldn't see eye to eye. There is such a thing as a positive personality clash. There can be two men, both of them fine individuals, sound in principle and well-intentioned, who nevertheless seem always to rub each other the wrong way, who seem never able to head in the same direction together. They get along splendidly with everyone else, but they grate on each other. But I think that such personality clashes are rare—and I think that bishops wisely try to correct such situations when they occur. However, if we do find ourselves in such a situation and until it *is* corrected, Christ has a right to expect us to exercise the heroic self-discipline that may be demanded of us in order to preserve the spirit of peace and harmony. Incidentally, when we talk of natural antipathies, we are not talking of that disagreeable individual who is chronically at odds with everyone. With such a one, it is not a matter of natural antipathy, it is a matter of overweening pride and self-love.

But it is neither natural antipathies nor the incurable malcontents that account for the tensions that exist (at least occasionally) in so many rectories. And if I dare to touch lightly upon some of them, I beg my readers to remember that I have been both an assistant and a pastor and now am neither; I should be able to bring a certain degree of objectivity to the subject.

First of all there is the age-old conflict between youth and enthusiasm, on the one hand, and age and experience on the other. It is a conflict that I presume would exist in any walk of life. A young doctor working under a veteran physician probably would consider the old man to be out-dated, slow and stodgy, maybe even lazy—and dictatorial to boot. The graybeard in turn would perhaps look upon the youngster as being brash, impudent, and an unreliable enthusiast. The same would be true of a pair of lawyers or a pair of mechanics—especially if they had to live together as well as work together.

So we start out together, pastor and assistant, under that universal handicap of disparity of age. Then further complications enter the picture. We come from the seminary (I say "we" because I am harking back now to my own youth)—we come from the seminary after several years spent in an environment in which we are protected and dependent. They are the very years when other young men are trying their wings, learning to stand on their own feet, and achieving emotional maturity. We have missed the seasoning process that most young men living in the world already have gone through. As a consequence (and let us be honest enough to admit it), often we come from the seminary still emotionally immature. Many of the normal conflicts of adolescence are still ahead of us—the conflicts that result from youth's urge for independence, on the one hand, and an unrecognized desire for security on the other.

Sometimes we start to catch up on our missed youth. We feel a sense of exhilaration as we plunge into all the young people's activities. We coach the athletic teams if we can, or at least sit on the bench with the players. We love to dawdle in the dairy bar with the younger set, and take in their parties if we can manage it. We have been going to bed by bells for years, but now life doesn't begin until after dark, and it's wonderful to be able to turn in when we please. Pushing doorbells on parish visitation is unadventurous drudgery; but we are willing to make the sacrifice so long as we are allowed generous time for our skating and swimming and hot-rodding and all the other things we've been missing for so long.

Our pastor seems a fussy old bird who acts as though he were afraid to trust us out of his sight. He seems to spend half his time thinking up things for us to do, and checking up on us to see whether we've done them. The other half of the time he seems mostly to just sit doodling at his desk, or talking interminably with old women in his office or old cronies in his study. We wouldn't mind doing most of the work (we tell ourselves), if only he didn't give us all the hard and disagreeable jobs; if only he didn't keep throwing cold water on all the good ideas we propose for the improvement of things around the parish and for the salvation of souls. The picture is a bit overdrawn, but it is a pretty good description of myself a quarter-century ago.

Of course, all assistants aren't young men, unfortunately. I say unfortunately because I do feel that it is something of a tragedy that in some dioceses men have to spend twenty or twenty-five years in the priesthood before getting parishes of their own. Little by little the drive and energy of youth languish, without the spur of responsibility to replace them. Unless a man has developed a very deep spiritual life for himself, he is in danger of becoming a mere timeserver in his later years as an assistant. When he does get a parish, he may be the very kind of pastor who will drive his assistants crazy. It is a pet theory of my own (and perhaps is out of place here) that it would be far better for all concerned if we had fewer large parishes and more small neighborhood parishes. Four pastors in four small parishes will do more good for souls, normally, than one pastor and three assistants in a big parish.

But that is beside the present point. The question now is (having disposed of the assistants) what complications do pastors contribute to parish tensions? First of all, I do not think that laziness is a notable factor. We do slow up physically as we get older; either we slow up or we die young. But pastors still work. As the assistant starts out on his round of census calls and sees (perhaps with a bit of resentment) the pastor sitting at his desk, the young man cannot know how much time is involved just in the physical administration of a parish plant. I do not think anyone can know that until he has been a pastor himself. Repairs to be arranged for, plans to be made, salesmen and contractors to be seen, janitors and housekeepers and school staffs to be consulted and mollified or goaded.

The old lady in the parlor may be crying her heart out because of her drinking husband; or maybe it's the Altar Society president, whose labors have helped to pay off half the parish debt, who now seems to be helping the pastor waste his time. The old crony in the study perhaps is boring the pastor to death, with Christian charity admitting of no escape; or he may be a man whose advice on building the pastor finds invaluable. I will not say that there are no lazy pastors; I will just say that I do not know many.

But perhaps pastors too could sometimes do a better job of contributing to the unity of parish life. I think that we may be much too fearful about trusting initiative to young assistants. They will make mistakes, certainly, but the world will not come to an end. We have made our own share of mistakes. In fact, that probably accounts for our timorousness in letting our assistants have their head. We are afraid they may pull the same boners we did, only maybe worse. It's very much like an experienced motorist teaching a beginner to drive. The beginner isn't worried at all; but the teacher is aware every moment of all the hazards that lurk on the highway, of all the power that is in the throttle, and comes back from the driving lesson a nervous wreck while the pupil is chipper as a sparrow. But, whether in a car or in a parish, the beginner has to go out on his own some time; he'll learn, the way we did, the things that no one can tell him.

We do, too, as we grow older, lose our enthusiasm to a great extent. If we do not exactly become cynical, at least we do develop a certain "*cui bono?*" attitude towards new plans and experiments. We have tried so many things ourselves in the course of years, and so few of them proved of any value, that we are tempted to view with a bilious eye the latest grand project of the ebullient assistant. But it is just possible that he may succeed where we have failed; we have nothing to lose by letting him try and giving him an encouraging word and an honest prayer for his success. God will decide the outcome.

Another fault that we pastors are prone to is the tendency to become too possessive as we grow older. The rectory becomes "my" home, and I look upon the assistant almost as a transient boarder. The parish is "my" parish and these are "my" people. Almost I feel that the assistant has no right to do anything in my parish or with my people unless he tells me all about it before and after—any more than he has a right to be entertaining his company in my home.

The parish of course *is* primarily my responsibility, before God and my bishop. But I do need to go all out in sharing responsibility with my assistants, trying to make of the rectory staff a unified team; consulting together, planning together, sharing together—with myself merely the senior member of the team. A rectory should never become a disunified aggregation of individuals, the boss and the underlings, with domination and grudging subservience in frequent conflict.

The matter of sharing, I think, should include sharing the rectory, which ought to be the home of *all* the priests who live there. Even a convent will have a parlor where a sister may entertain her guests, apart from the superior's office. Every rectory, too, should have a room where the assistants may entertain their family or friends, apart from the pastor's appraising eye.

Then there is the problem of the housekeeper. I hesitate to touch upon the subject, for fear that I may seem to do injustice to that great group of noble women who, like the holy women who ministered to Christ, also live their lives in obscurity and selfless labor, caring for Christ's priests. The appreciation they receive is seldom proportionate to the sacrifices they make; I am sure there must be a very choice spot for them in Heaven.

But they are human, as we are human. It is the pastor who hires the housekeeper, it is the pastor who pays her; and it is only human to give first place to the man who signs your pay check. But beyond that, as a housekeeper spends years in the service of a pastor, he becomes her one secure anchor in an uncertain world. Her maternal instincts have been poured out upon him until in time she develops a proprietary interest in the good Father. Assistants come and go. To the housekeeper they may seem irresponsible boys who just make more work for her without any compensatory consolations. All this is very natural—but it also can be very tough on the assistants.

The wise pastor will from the very beginning maintain a priestly reserve with his housekeeper, so that she may never become that bane of a parish, the queen dowager of the rectory. Ninety-nine and nine-tenths per cent of our housekeepers are exemplary women who *want* to do the right thing and maintain the right attitude in the rectory—if only the pastor will provide unobtrusive guidance in the beginning. I don't like to use the phrase "keeping the housekeeper in her place"; it sounds too snobbish. But it is essential that a clear line be drawn between the work of the house and the work of the parish—with the work of the parish handled only by the priests. It is not for me to lay down rules; but I will offer the opinion that a pastor should never relay orders or instructions to his assistant through the housekeeper. I do not think either that the housekeeper should sit at table with the priests (where there is more than one) nor with them in their common room. This again is not snobbishness; it simply is that the priests of the parish have little enough time together; if they want to discuss parish business or priestly affairs, there should be no compulsion to wariness of speech because of the housekeeper's presence. In short, no assistant should ever have to play second fiddle to the housekeeper, saintly and capable soul though she may be. Not even if she is the pastor's own mother or sister.

We could go on, discussing other sources of pastor-assistant tension within our rectories. But let us end it all by admitting that such tensions, when they do exist, are just surface symptoms of a fundamental lack: a lack of that true charity, that deep love for each other in Christ, which the Master so fervently besought for us on Holy Thursday night. No matter what natural differences there may be in age or personality or function—a supernatural love can surmount them all. There never can be *complete* unity unless and until each is willing to surrender a little of himself to the other. But that is no excuse for any individual holding back. Even one man alone can do much to mend the breach in the unity-in-love which ought to be found, above all places, in the home where priests dwell together. Even one man can make a start towards answering Christ's prayer, "That all may be one, even as Thou, Father, in Me and I in Thee; that the world may believe that Thou hast sent Me."

THE UNSECULAR PRIEST

IT IS A PITY that in an age when the dominant heresy is that of Secularism, in a day when the word "secularist" is a pejorative tag—it is a pity that the diocesan clergy should be handicapped with the title of "secular" priests. We know the honorable origin of the term. We know that we are called seculars because we live in the world rather than in the cloister. But there remains enough of a sting in the name to make most of us prefer what is, factually, a much more accurate classification: that of "diocesan" priests. I say that it is a much more accurate term because, after all, the place where we live—rectory versus monastery—is much less specific a mark of differentiation than is the object of our immediate obedience— a bishop rather than a religious superior.

But whether we like it or not, it seems that we are stuck with the designation of "seculars." It remains for us to make certain that when applied to us, the name "secular" never means more than it is intended to mean; that it means solely and exclusively those who live *in* the world; and never, so far as we are concerned, those who live on easy terms *with* the world.

In this latter sense of the word, we must strive and

struggle to be thoroughly *un*secular priests. Christ Himself made the distinction very clear-cut for us when He prayed for us on Holy Thursday night. "I pray for them," He said to His Father; "for those whom Thou hast given Me. . . . I am no longer in the world, but these are in the world. . . . I do not pray that Thou take them out of the world, but that Thou keep them from evil. They are not of the world, even as I am not of the world."

It *is* a strife and a struggle to keep ourselves unworldly, unsecular. By the very fact that we do live *in* the world, we are continually exposed to the steady pressure of its thrust. A vague and general intention to have no part in worldliness is not enough. Day by day, by repeated voluntary acts, we must beat back its well-concealed compulsion.

We know that the world itself is not essentially bad— nor the things and the people in the world. All things that are, were made by God, and therefore are essentially good. Jesus Christ redeemed the world and all things in it from the dominion of Satan. But Christ did *not* destroy the freedom of human wills which His Father from the beginning had bestowed. It is the turning of the human will away from God or against God that makes a good man bad. It is the loving of a creature to the exclusion of God that makes an objectively good thing subjectively bad. It is this act of violent and fundamental disorder, this perversity of human wills, that turns to evil the essential goodness of God's creation—a creation whose final as well as formal cause is the glorification of God Himself.

We recall that just to set the record straight. When we talk of the world, worldliness, the spirit of the world, we are not talking of the world in the abstract, the world of things and men as God made them. We are talking of the world as it is used and directed by free human wills; by human wills which have largely forgotten or which ignore their ultimate and eternal destiny. We are talking of a world in which temporal well-being is too often made an end in itself—the ultimate as well as a proximate end of human effort and human wisdom.

We do not condemn the world *as* world, any more than we would condemn a house *as* house simply because it was a house of prostitution. To eliminate the evil of the bordello we would not burn down the house—we would try to convert the inhabitants. Similarly it is our duty as priests, indeed our duty as *Christians,* not to shut ourselves away from the world while the world destroys itself. It is our duty rather to be malleable, responsive instruments in the hand of Christ as He continues—and will continue to the end—His work of redemption, of transformation, of redirection to God.

It scarcely needs pointing out that we shall not be effective as redemptive agents of Christ if we ourselves are *of* the world. You cannot pull someone up unless you stand on higher ground yourself. You cannot lead another forward unless you yourself are a little in advance. You cannot flavor water by pouring more water in. Or, as Jesus put it even more graphically and concisely, "If the salt loses its savor, wherewith shall it be salted?"

We must then be unworldly priests. And we must avoid the easy error of over-estimating our own unworldliness. Not a single one of us is completely unworldly, as unworldly as we can and ought to be. The secular spirit is like an odorless, colorless, all-pervasive vapor. We cannot exaggerate its penetrative power. It will be a miracle of grace if we do not breathe some of it in.

It is an elementary observation to note that the antidote to worldliness is a spirit of detachment. The spirit of detachment, in turn, is simply a matter of keeping things in their right perspective, keeping a right order to our hierarchy of values. Getting down to particulars and examining ourselves on our own resistance to worldliness, we might say that the measure of our detachment lies in our attitude towards people and things. Since "attitude" may seem a word of indeterminate meaning, let me cite a practical example of what it means in this context. For the purpose of my example I shall make use of two entirely imaginary priests, Father Smith and Father Jones. Both are pastors, both are good priests, genuinely interested in the welfare of their respective flocks.

Father Smith makes a call on a family in his parish whom he has heard of recently, a family who should be Catholics but who have made no appearance at church. He finds their home—a rather dilapidated house—and parks at the curb in front of it. His Chrysler car is bright and shiny, because Father Smith is very particular in the care he gives his car. The lady of the house answers his ring at the door, ushers him into the somewhat disordered living-room, and calls to her husband to come and meet the Father. The husband, just home from work and having a bottle of beer in the kitchen, comes in obediently and somewhat embarrassedly in his shirtsleeves. To the tune of the wife's inevitable apologies for the upset condition of her home, they all sit down.

Now, as the couple listen to Father Smith explain his

errand—and he does so in a kindly fashion (he is a good priest, a good pastor, or he wouldn't be making this call)—but as the couple listen, let us try to see Father Smith through their eyes. He is a well-groomed gentleman, really distinguished-looking in a quiet way. His graying hair is well cared for, neatly trimmed and every hair in place. His homburg (or is it a borsalino?) hat rests on his sharply creased knees. His suit fits with the perfection which only a first-class tailor can achieve; the only thing to mar its handsome contour is the bulge of the cigars in his breast-pocket. His shoes, of course, are polished with the sheen that really fine leather will take.

The couple facing Father Smith do not take note of any of the details, not consciously. They only sense in a confused sort of way that between this man, so impeccably groomed, so prosperous-looking against the background of his fine car glistening through the window—between him and them there is a gulf. He is on a different level from themselves, and they cannot expect him to understand their problems. So they are courteous to him, apologetic, even effusive. They promise that they will start coming to church. Actually they never do quite get around to acting on their promise before they have to move again.

In the new parish to which they move, there is another good shepherd, Father Jones. In the course of time he hears of the family and calls on them. He receives the same courteous treatment as did Father Smith, but with different results. Before Father Jones has finished his visit the atmosphere has grown very friendly, even cordial. The couple confide that they were never married by the priest, that their youngest child was never baptized. Before he leaves, the couple have made a definite date with Father Jones to come and arrange for the validation of their marriage and the baptism of their child. The oldest youngster will be started to catechism class right away, too. Things will be different from now on.

If you asked the couple why they found it so much easier to talk to Father Jones, they couldn't have told you; except maybe to say, "Well, somehow he seemed more like one of ourselves." There probably was no explicit awareness of the slight bagginess of his pants, of the lack-lustre of his shoes, of the fact that he was almost due for a hair-cut, of the fact that his somewhat dusty Chevvie looked so much at home in front of their house. None of these things would have registered individually, and yet the man in his sweaty work-shirt and the woman in her limp house-dress felt quite at ease with Father Jones.

Before there is a chorus of objections, let me say at once that I am not advocating a disheveled clergy, a deliberate affectation of sloppy clothes and scuffed shoes and collar-length hair. I am only trying to illustrate the fact that unworldliness is an attitude, a state of mind (or rather a state of heart?) which will inescapably reflect itself in a man's whole makeup. The unworldly priest will be clean and neat because it befits his dignity as man and priest—but still his cleanliness and neatness will be of secondary and even tertiary importance. Often he will be late in getting to the barber-shop, to the dry-cleaner's, to the car-wash because there are so many acts of duty or charity which make more insistent demands upon his time. He has the spirit of detachment: everything is appraised and valued in its relationship to God: is it essential, is it at least important, is it only desirable—or is it merely indifferent?

F

Here, then, are some straws in the wind that may help us in determining the degree of our own detachment: What about our own wardrobe? Is it the wardrobe of an average working-man—a change of suits so that we need not go naked while the dry-cleaner does his work, a change of shoes, such linens as we need—everything of decent but not superlative quality? Or are our clothespress and dresser drawers loaded with a variety of garments for every occasion, everything in abundance and everything of the very best?

An inventory of our other possessions will help us, too. How many *things* do we have that we do not really need? Do we buy books that we never read, and keep on our shelves books that will never be opened again? An expensive camera that we seldom use, and which serves us no better than a cheaper model would? A high-fidelity record-player of magnificent tone, with a stack of record albums second to none in our parish? A luxurious reclining lounge-chair that can be either a bed or a seat at the press of a button? A portable bar with a stock of the finest, and equipment for our favorite sport that a professional might envy?

I shan't try to exhaust the list here. But what about our food—does that assume undue importance in our lives? Is our taste finicky, do we shop for delicacies and insist upon certain dishes being prepared to our exacting taste? Do we delight in patronizing those discriminating restaurants where the prices are even richer than the food? Do we have a sense of gustatory discernment superior to that of a Duncan Hines?

Then, what about our travels and our vacations? Do we feel that we owe it to ourselves to "splurge" a bit, to seek the best hotels, the best accommodations of every kind, everywhere and always? Especially, does the yoke of our priesthood sit so gallingly upon us that we all but shuck it off during vacation, dressing in mufti and indulging in amusements that are perhaps not sinful, but hardly priestly?

Because of the absence of external pressures, there probably is no time like vacation for assaying the extent of our compromise with the spirit of the world. And for us priests, every compromise with the world is a spiritual Munich—leading not to peace but to increased conflict within ourselves. Trying to assuage our thirst for happiness with *things* is like trying to satisfy physical thirst with salt water.

The truly unworldly priest has a subconscious norm for every dollar he spends, even when those dollars come from some source outside his ministry. He can never quite forget the insatiable needs of Christ's Mystical Body: the missionary appeals on his desk for funds to build a chapel in India, to hire catechists in Africa, to establish a dispensary in Korea. He has docketed in his mind the homes in his parish where the parents are waging a desperate fight against inflation, perhaps against sickness and unemployment. He gets far more joy out of helping a poor student through the seminary than he could ever get out of a car with power steering and automatic shift.

So far we have been talking about things. However, persons also come into our purview of secularism. There is a danger (maybe not a big one, but it's there) which especially threatens us older prests, who are inclined to grow more conservative with the passing years. We can

rather easily develop the outlook of the successful business man and find ourselves too closely associated by
mentality with the country-club set.

I am not speaking now of the ambitious or self-seeking
priest who cultivates the friendship of upper-crust laity
for obviously selfish reasons—and who often is despised
by the very ones he seeks to cultivate. Nor am I referring
to the affection-seeking priest who mistakenly tries to
quiet the heart's desire with human love rather than with
divine love. Neither am I here envisioning the eternally
adolescent priest, who plunges into "youth work" not
merely as a spiritual guide and counsellor, but as an
active participant; trying to satisfy a yearning for the
boyish excitement missed in his own sheltered youth.

All of these are, true enough, species of human attach-
ments. But they do not stem quite so clearly from the
spirit of secularism as the type of attachment in which
the priest seems to have absorbed what we might call
Chamber-of-Commerce attitudes and preferences. I do
not mean to belittle the layman who is a member of the
Chamber of Commerce. I mean only to question whether
a priest may not greatly limit his priestly effectiveness,
who becomes too intimate with the business, industrial
and political tycoons of his community. This particular
priest is not looking for anything for himself; he honestly
does find such companionship congenial—because his own
mental outlook has taken on a secularistic tinge. I have
known priests (and I emphasize that they were *good*
priests) who could wax as eloquent on the abuses and
irresponsibilities of the labor unions as could the most
reactionary employer. I have known priests who have
extended aid to the needy, not with the compassion of
Christ, not with the sense of guilt that we all ought to

have in the presence of poverty—but with something close to contempt for the so-called shiftlessness of the poor. I have known priests whose views on racial justice were akin to those of a dweller in an exclusive suburb: "We have to move slowly in these things. Theory is all right, but we have to be practical, we have to think of property-values. Let the Negro prove himself first, and *deserve* equality."

These are just quick and random snapshots of a priest who has let himself be influenced by the spirit of secularism. If we find in none of them an actual likeness to ourselves, perhaps we may catch here and there a fugitive glimpse of a feature which does have a slight similarity to the man we know best—something which distorts just a little the perfect picture of what we ought to be: priests in the image and after the Heart of Christ.

I hope you will understand that I am not saying that a priest should throw out everything in his quarters except a straight-back chair and a pine table for his study, and an iron cot with straw mattress for his bedroom. I do not believe that Christ will object to us having the ordinary comforts and conveniences such as the people have among whom we labor. Nor would He object to us having any of the modern machines and inventions which will add to the efficacy of our work. The point is that a fully unsecular priest upon walking into newly assigned quarters would not particularly notice or care whether he had a pine table or a mahogany desk, whether he had an innerspring mattress or a cotton tick. He would neither throw anything out nor be moved to add anything unnecessary; he just wouldn't *care*, so long as he could function as a priest.

So, when we undertake to appraise the extent to which

the spirit of worldliness has influenced us, I do not think it is enough for us to be able to say, "I would give this up in a minute if it were necessary, if God asked me to." That, of course, is a basic attitude towards worldly goods—things or people—which every Christian must have. But true detachment goes farther than this. In assaying the things we possess, the hobbies we adopt, the recreations we indulge in, the non-clerical friendships we form, the true spirit of detachment will ask: "Does this, from Christ's viewpoint, make sense as a part of my priestly life? Does it in some way, even indirectly, enable me to function better as a pastor of souls? Am I sure that it in no way dims my likeness to my Master? Can I be certain that I would experience no embarrassment in explaining it, if Christ Himself were to ask me for the reason for it?"

If we ask those questions of ourselves in all honesty, we may discover a little uneasiness of conscience here and there. (Let me confess that I am not wholly easy in my own conscience, even as I write the questions.) They are questions that we need to ask ourselves fairly frequently if we are going to continue, undiscouraged, our attempts to confine the meaning of the term "secular priest" to its original connotation. Because, just as the boiling-point of water is reached more quickly as the altitude increases, so too is the conflict between the goods of the world and the goods of the spirit reached more noticeably as we try, as all of us *must* try, to climb a little higher on the hill that is topped by the Cross of Christ.

THE CATHOLIC PRIEST

IT IS INTERESTING to note what disparate secondary meanings words can acquire. For example, the word "provincial." It is a very respectable adjective when used in its true and original meaning: "of or pertaining to a province." Certainly a Canadian would not feel offended if he were described as a Provincial legislator or a Provincial policeman. But it can be a very damning word when some sweet young thing says to her parent, "O Dad, don't be so provincial!" It has come to mean someone who is ultra-conservative, behind the times, not knowing what goes on in the big centers of thought and fashion. Having seen something of big cities and knowing some of the things that happen there, I myself would not feel in the least offended if I were called "provincial." The pendulum of semantics has swung so far that the word now is almost synonymous with "respectable."

But I think that I should feel somewhat disturbed if someone called me a "parochial" priest. Even though I might be a pastor with a parochial school and active parochial organizations, I still should feel uneasy if someone remarked, "But he's so *parochial!*" Because "parochial" has come to have that secondary meaning: one of limited vision; one who cannot see beyond his own narrow boundaries; one whose interests are confined to his own circumscribed field of action. In that sense, none of us should wish to be called a *"parochial"* priest.

We have a right to feel a holy and a grateful (Thank you, God) pride in the fact that we are *parish* priests, priests of the people, close to the people, working with and among them. But an even more glorious title is that of "Catholic" priest. Catholic, not only in its acquired meaning as a distinction between ourselves and priests of the Orthodox or the Anglican churches, but more than this: catholic priests with a small "c"; priests whose eyes can travel beyond the confines of our own parish, our own diocese, our own nation; priests whose vision is as wide as the sweeping gaze of Peter and his successors, as wide as the gaze of Christ; catholic in the sense of universal—for all, and everywhere.

Many of us have read such books as those of the Abbé Michonneau *(Revolution in a City Parish* and *The Missionary Spirit in Parish Life);* such books as Claire Bishop's *France Alive* and the powerful pastorals of Cardinal Suhard. But it should not take books such as these to make us realize that the Church of Christ is by its very nature a *missionary* Church. We are accustomed to distinguishing between the diocesan clergy and the home missionaries and the foreign missionaries. But every one of us is a missionary priest, a catholic priest with a small "c" because we are Catholic priests with a big "C".

Jesus placed no limitation of place or time or personnel when he gave His official charge to all of us, His priests: "Go, therefore, and make disciples of all nations"; "Go into the whole world and preach the Gospel to every creature!" In the degree to which we lose our sense of *mission*, our consciousness of being *sent* to all the world, our apostolic fervor—in that degree does the faith that we profess and preach lose its dynamism, to that degree does the Church languish and decline.

I think that it is unfortunate that the distinction between the parish clergy and the missionary clergy was ever introduced. What, after all, is the difference between you and me, and the priest in India or Africa? Each of us was sent to preach the Gospel and administer the sacraments in a certain well-defined territory. The priest in India or Africa may have a larger territory than ours; he may have a much higher proportion of unbelievers to believers than you or I have. But his responsibility is the same as yours and mine. None of us was sent merely to shepherd an established flock and to shut ourselves tightly within the fold with our sheep— all good sheep inside and nothing but wolves outside.

If we happened to hear of a priest who was sent to the African Gold Coast and who settled down to minister (however zealously) to the existing Christians, with no thought or feeling of responsibility to the thousands of pagans around him—well, we should be tempted to mild disgust, to say the least. And yet isn't that exactly what we, all too often, do? And why should our sin be any less than his? A parish isn't intended to be a closed and cozy circle of initiates clustered around a benign father, drowsing their way through time until the grand morning of eternity dawns. We are *missionaries*, Fathers; we are missionaries, every mother's son of us who has received the Sacrament of Holy Orders. Either we are missionaries, or we are not wholly Christ's.

We can test our own missionary spirit rather easily.

We have only to ask ourselves (and to honestly answer)
two questions: What am I doing for the lax, the fallen-
away, and the non-Catholics in my territory? What am
I doing for the Church as a whole? I know that some
will be tempted to answer both questions by saying,
"I'm doing all that I can; I'm so busy already just with
the routine work of running my parish that I feel sometimes like I'm on a treadmill. All this fancy talk about
being a missionary sounds fine, but let's be practical."
At least, that is the answer that I have given myself at
times, and in all sincerity, too.

And in giving the answer, of course, I was not being
truly catholic, truly apostolic. I was looking upon myself as being the *only* missionary in my territory, as the
one who must do it all. I was seeing my present flock
as the whole or main object of my labors, instead of
seeing them as helpers, auxiliaries, fellow missionaries.
So long as I did not accept the missionary role myself,
I could not of course imbue them with a missionary
spirit. As a consequence, much of the apostolic grace
and power that was theirs by virtue of Baptism and
Confirmation slumbered and was stultified.

We hesitate, so many of us, to share our responsibility
with the laity; or it would be more correct to say that
we hesitate to let them exercise the responsibility which
is theirs by reason of their Christian vocation. Instead
of firing them with a missionary spirit and enlisting them
with ourselves as a missionary team, we want them to
remain passive and obedient children. And there is so
much that they could do. They can make house-to-
house visitation, and carry on a pamphlet apostolate.
They can recruit members for the Inquiry Class. Some,
if they have the knowledge and the preparation, can

even give lectures to the Inquiry Class. They can gather in children for catechism class, especially from lax homes; and they can teach catechism to the children. They can visit the sick and aid the delinquent and organize maternity guilds and credit unions and co-operatives. There is so *much* they can do. Indeed, in a fully missionary parish the pastor's function would be limited to the spiritual formation of his helpers and the administration of the sacraments.

You will notice that I am not using the words "Catholic Action." I do not want to confuse the issue, even though "Catholic Action" is the term that the last two Holy Fathers have been using emphatically, over and over again. But it may keep the whole thing simpler if we just talk about the missionary vocation of the laity, the apostolate of the laity. It is a vocation which the Holy Father did not originate, let us remember; it is not an apostolate which stems from the condescension of you or me. It is a God-given apostolate. You and I may impart the spirit, we may stir up the fire; but the power and the responsibility and the grace are already there.

Why do we hesitate to let the laity have a greater share in the missionary work of the Church? Is it because we are afraid that they may get out of hand, that they may take too much upon themselves, that they may try to take things out of the hands of the priests and bishops? No, Fathers; not if they have the kind of spiritual formation and guidance which it is our part to give. We know our Church History. We know that from Arius through Luther and Calvin it so often has been clerics, rather than laymen, who have made the gaping tears in the seamless robe of Christ.

If the priests in India, Africa, Japan, Malaya followed

the system of trying to do it all themselves, how meager would be their fruit. With them, every convert becomes another missionary. Christian teaches pagan, who becomes Christian, and the chain goes on and on, as the flame of the faith is passed from hand to hand. Their laity may be but one generation removed from paganism, but they do not worry about sects and defections. Can we be less willing to trust our own laity, whose faith is as ancient as our own?

Let me make a confession. Any time that I have found myself—well, squirming a bit—at the apostolic zeal and action of the laity, I have been able to trace my discomfort to one cause only: I have had to run too fast to keep up with them. They have shamed my own easy-going ways. They have made demands upon my own spiritual resources and have made me conscious of my spiritual inadequacies and sloth. I have sighed after the flesh-pots of leisure and tranquility, and for a fleeting moment have regretted getting myself involved in such a Christian and pentecostal activity.

Assuming, however, that we are truly catholic priests, with an interest and zeal that extends to *all* the souls within our territory, not merely to those already baptized in the Faith; assuming (as we must) that the priest alone and unaided is unable to accomplish much of his missionary vocation; assuming, finally, that we are catholic priests to the degree that we want to utilize *all* the means at our disposal for the Christianization of the world, particularly the God-given missionary talents and graces of our laity—assuming all this, what in practice can a catholic priest do? Good will granted, what are some of the tools available?

First of all there is the Confraternity of Christian

Doctrine. It may seem incongruous to be recommending the Confraternity of Christian Doctrine to priests, when canon law already prescribes that this Confraternity be erected in every parish. But observation will tell us that there are many parishes, and perhaps some dioceses, where the Confraternity of Christian Doctrine either does not exist at all or exists only in a rudimentary and ineffective form.

Yet here is the missionary training school and the missionary vehicle, par excellence, for our people. How many of us, I wonder, are familiar with the Confraternity set-up—the scope of its program, the aids that it offers? There are the Confraternity Religious Discussion Clubs, adaptable to any kind of parish, in which the members not only grow in a knowledge of their faith, but learn how to put that faith to work for others. There is the Confraternity method of recruiting and training the laity to teach religion to children. There are Confraternity members who devote their apostolic talent to the visiting of lax Catholic homes and the enrollment of children in religious instruction classes; still other Confraternity members will provide transportation for such children who live at a distance. There is no project involving the spread of Christian truth which is alien to the Confraternity of Christian Doctrine. Where it is solidly established in a parish, with active guidance and above all with truly spiritual direction from the pastor—in that parish the priest has multiplied his effectiveness a hundredfold.

Take only the parish Inquiry Class, which is providentially coming into wider and wider use as a means of extending the Kingdom of Christ. It is easy to start an Inquiry Class, just by announcing from the altar that on such-and-such an evening, the Inquiry Class will begin.

But there is a tremendous amount of work involved in having a *successful* Inquiry Class: one which begins with a satisfactory enrollment of non-Catholics, continues fruitfully to the end, and continues to repeat itself with equal effectiveness through the year and through the years. There is so much groundwork to be laid, in the way of promotion and publicity and good-will. There is so much follow-up to be done, in the way of continued contacts and integration of the new members into the parish community. There is so much need, particularly in one-priest parishes, of auxiliary lecturers who can carry the class along when inevitable emergencies prevent the pastor's presence. All of these things the members of the parish Confraternity can do, and it is but one example of what they can do. Strengthened by the feeling of corporateness which membership in the Confraternity gives, fortified by the graces and indulgences which his membership brings, made confident by the helps and the directives which it provides, the layman is able to uncork the apostolic power and the missionary dynamism which are inherent to the Faith in which he has been baptized and confirmed.

A newer organization, but one which is exhibiting vigorous power wherever it is established, is the Legion of Mary. It combines a strong spiritual program for the personal formation of its members with a wide program of action to which none of the works of mercy are alien. The fact that missionaries in foreign lands are finding the *Legio Mariae* such a forceful auxiliary arm to themselves should make us missionaries at home realize its potentialities as a focus for Christian and apostolic leadership in our own parishes. Again, the only demand upon the priest will be for strong spiritual direction and priestly guidance. In the layman, as in the priest, the apostolic spirit cannot thrive upon pabulum; a strong spirit needs strong food. Just as the non-praying and the non-penitential priest is a weak priest, so is the non-praying and non-penitential layman a passive conformist.

The Sodality of Our Lady is another organization with great possibilities as a missionary force. It already exists in many parishes, but too often it is only a pale replica of the apostolic organism that it is designed to be. How many of us, I wonder, have ever made a serious study of the Sodality Rule? How many of us who have Sodalities give our Candidates the thorough novitiate that the Probation period envisions—the radical training that they need if they are to understand, fully accept, and live by their duties as Sodalists. When they make their solemn Act of Consecration they pledge themselves to daily Mass and daily meditation, among other things. Are they ready for that? Do they fully understand what it means to sanctify themselves, to sanctify others, to defend the Church? So often the Sodality Rule is soft-pedaled and watered down for the sake of enlisting large numbers; whereas the Holy Father himself urges that the Sodality be a band of spiritually elite, vigorously apostolic souls. A Sodality not infrequently is an active group of good wholesome Catholic young people—but the activity is a piddling sort of activity—not the vital *missionary* activity that can and should flow from the Sodality.

Another organization, one of very recent vintage and at present confined pretty much to the United States, is the Christian Family Movement—the CFM to its familiars. I hesitate, really, to call it an organization, because it is more in the nature of a co-operative federation of groups of married couples. Parish groups—and there can be several groups in a parish—are made up of married couples who work towards the Christianization of their own families and of the environment in which they live: their own neighborhood, their own community, their own parish. Such groups are established only with the approval of the pastor and under his spiritual direction, or with the spiritual guidance of a priest designated by him. They determine upon, discuss, and act upon their common problems as Christian families. The steady and unpressured growth of the Christian Family Movement during the past three or four years is the best recommendation of its inherent worth. In view of the basic importance of genuinely Christian family life to the health and Christian growth of any community, any pastor interested in the upbuilding of a truly missionary parish would do well to investigate the possibilities of the CFM.[1]

There has been no attempt here to provide an exhaustive list of apostolic organizations—those which, when properly directed, will fan the missionary spirit of their members. Thank God the list is too long to admit of that. These have been offered simply as samples, as some of the top samples, of the distilled wisdom and experience that is available to any priest whose vision extends beyond the purely parochial care of his own immediate flock.

After all, the name of the organization does not matter too much—except for the strength that the members will find in their sense of corporateness. Nor does the organization itself matter too much, except insofar as its program may hasten faltering steps, and obviate the mistakes that are inherent in any trial-by-error method. What does matter is that we priests ourselves become imbued with the conviction of the missionary nature of our own voca-

[1] The Headquarters address, for any who may be interested, is 100 West Monroe Street, Room 2010, Chicago 3, Illinois.

tion, so that there will no longer be a valid distinction between parish priests and missionary priests, but only between parish missionaries and foreign missionaries.

It matters, too, that we feel dissatisfied with what we have done for our own people, unless and until their personal sanctification begins to bear fruit in a strong sense of missionary responsibility, begins to seek outlet in some form of apostolic activity with an urgency that will not be denied. That means raising their spiritual temperature several degrees beyond the usually accepted level. It means that we cannot be content with a parish of Sunday Mass-goers seasoned with a sprinkling of devotees. We must aim at nothing less than a parish of saints. We may never achieve it, but on the other hand we dare never to be content with less.

The whole world is a mission field, and will be to the end; your parish and mine, as well as Asia and Africa and Russia. As soon as we slack off, something will rush in to fill the vacuum; Protestantism in the sixteenth century, Communism today. And just as the condemnation of Luther by the Diet of Augsburg in 1530 did not stop the rise of Protestantism, so neither will mere condemnation —nor witch-hunting nor book-burnings—stop Communism today. Communism has its dogmas and its mystique; above all, it has an internal dynamism that makes apostles of its followers. We shall only defeat Communism to the degree that we combat the dogmas of Marx with the fully understood truths of Christ, the mystique of Lenin with the asceticism of Christ—above all, the dynamism of Communism with the irresistible dynamism of the Gospel of Christ. We can't do that alone. To make of our laity saints and missionaries; that, as I see it, is our task today.

THE ALERT PRIEST

THE OLDER generation of priests who have been out of the seminary for a quarter of a century or more will remember one point in pastoral theology that always was gravely emphasized: the need for a priest to develop a love for study, so that in the long lonely hours he might expect to face he might not dessicate in idleness, or be tempted to frivolous dissipation or worse.

For most of us, those long lonely hours have never developed. We came out of the seminary just as the more leisurely and simple life of yesterday was breathing its last. The automobile and good roads; electricity and rapid communication; the great corporations and the unions; a higher standard of living and of education; the birth of modern advertising and its creation of a whole new galaxy of wants and desires: these phenomena and a host of others have been witnessed by those of us who are over fifty. By this network of social, economic and physical factors the tempo of life has been increased ten-fold, the tension of living stepped up immeasurably.

The concept of leisure as a time for gracious living, a time for self-improvement and self-realization, has all but disappeared. There is plenty of recreation, but recreation itself has become institutionalized, commercialized. To-day a family cannot decide what they are going to do on a Sunday or a holiday until first they have scanned the newspaper. What will it be: the horse races or the auto races; the big-league baseball game or the movies; the hockey game or the pro football game; the ice-show or the aquacade; the builder's show or the sportsmen's show; or shall we just stay at home and watch television?

Now I would not have you think that I am a *"laudator temporis act"* mumbling in his beard about the good old days. The world will not stand still, and time has brought much that is good as well as much that is questionable. But it all adds up to a very busy world, the world in which you and I live, whose influence we cannot wholly escape. It is our responsibility as priests, indeed it is our duty as Christians, to labor to preserve the permanent values of life in spite of the turbulence around us.

One of those values is what I have called self-improvement or self-realization. Whatever it may be called matters little. What it *is*, is the continuing development of our God-given powers: the enrichment and growth of our minds, the perfecting of our talents, the maturing of our judgment, the discovery and utilization of some un-suspected aptitude; in short, the rounding out of the whole man (and I am not referring to waistlines).

This urge to self-realization is latent in every human being. Its satisfaction is one of the richest sources of natural happiness. But we as Christians, besides being destined by nature to the augmentation and full utilization of our faculties, have a *supernatural* obligation to develop and use the talents that God has given us; and as priests, because so many others will profit by every increase in ourselves, for us the obligation is doubly pressing. In our effectiveness as priests, the truth is that either we grow or we wither; either we ripen or we rot.

Priests, and in particular parish priests, are busy men. Because there is a certain minimum of things which *have* to be done whose doing cannot be escaped, even the lazy ones among us (if there are any) would be adjudged by union standards to have earned their modest salaries by the end of the week. But, since it is for God and not for a salary that we work; since the task of saving souls is of an urgency which permits no weighing of the cost in time or pain; since nothing less than the full giving of ourselves to God will merit His commendation, "Well done, thou good and faithful servant"; since we must be able to say with our heart as well as our lips, "The zeal of Thy house hath eaten me up!"—we shall do well to ask ourselves, "What do I do with such spare time as I have?"

With some of us, I know, there will be days that are so crowded with duty that we have difficulty squeezing in our meals. But for most of us and on most days there are interludes between tasks that would add up to a larger total than we are likely to realize. The world has so many little leeches spread around, waiting greedily to gobble up such odd moments of leisure as may come to us. There is the daily newspaper, with its headlines giving false importance to events that will be forgotten tomorrow, with its comic page which seems to say that life should be frittered, not lived, away. There on the end-table are the secular magazines—slick, witty, sophisticated; viewing the world and man and all things else (including basic truths and principles) with an easy tolerance; seducing our interest with an appeal that has been calculated to the last footnote of mass-psychology. There in the corner is the radio; or, more alluring still, the television—which by mere motion can mesmerize us and can conjure away the good that in this hour or half or quarter we thought we were going to do. Then, of course, there is always the bed. It may not be lack of sleep that makes us drowsy; it may be a lunch that was too hearty or blood that is too sluggish. It may not be the distance we have traveled that makes us weary; it may be the excess fat that we are carrying around. But of course the siren mattress will remind us of none of these things as it invites us to its embrace.

We know that none of these things are bad. They are gifts of God and are to be accepted with becoming gratitude—but they are to be used with temperance. It is one thing to say, at the end of a day that has driven us hard, "I'm completely fagged, mentally as well as physically; what I need is an hour of light reading or a good TV show to let my nerves unwind." It is another thing to dibble-dabble throughout the day and evening at time-killing devices, whenever an imperative task does not push us forcefully into activity.

It is one thing to welcome our weekly day-off as an integral and re-creative part of our schedule, and to spend the day in wholesome enjoyment with our family or our priest friends. It is another thing to become so addicted to golf or bowling or fishing, to wood-working or electronics, that we are constantly looking for every minute that we can garner to satisfy our personal tastes. Hobbies have a place in the scheme of things and can even contribute to making us better priests. But it is bad when a man begins to build his life around his hobby, instead of fitting the hobby into his life.

First of all we realize that we must do some serious

reading. Not necessarily spiritual reading always, but reading with a purpose, reading that will add to our effectiveness as priests. Our clerical reviews, for example, always will take precedence over *Collier's* or the *Saturday Evening Post;* one or two of the better Catholic magazines will come before *Life* or *Look.* A book on parish administration, or on convert-making, or on the theology of the Mass, or on the liturgy, or on Christian sociology—books such as these will be more frequently in our hands than murder mysteries or even religious novels. And if I may digress for a moment to be even more specific, I think that books on the family and its problems and on mental hygiene should be much more widely read by us today, to fit us better for the task of extra-confessional counselling which seems to be increasingly a part of our pastoral work.

Just as our reading should be, in the main, pastorally profitable reading, so too should our principal hobby be of a type that will extend our priestly usefulness. An eminent churchman has said that any priest who shoots more than ninety in golf is neglecting his game, and any priest who shoots below ninety is neglecting his parish. The prelate in question is a golfer himself, of course; but I think that the same principle would apply to any avocation. Any time that a priest becomes too proficient at any activity that lies outside the field of his priesthood—whether it be skill at sleight-of-hand or raising guppy fish—souls are being neglected. Not consciously perhaps, but souls still are being neglected. (And you will understand that I am not talking about priest-scientists or priest professors whose exceptional apostolate may have exceptional needs; I am talking about priest-missioners, such as the great majority of us are.)

I said that our principal hobby should be of a type that will extend our priestly usefulness. Maybe what I have in mind cannot be called a hobby at all—but it would be a supra-parochial activity that would widen our interests, enlist our hidden talents, and satisfy that innate craving which all of us have, a craving that is natural and not to be condemned—the desire to attain some measure of worthwhile achievement. We can accomplish all this, I think, by actively interesting ourselves in some one of the specialized movements in which the Church abounds, movements in which informed and vigorous priestly leadership never reaches the saturation point.

There is, for example, in the United States the National Catholic Rural Life Conference with its headquarters at Des Moines, Iowa. For the priest in a rural community particularly, active participation in the work of the Conference should be a rewarding and a satisfying experience. The National Catholic Rural Life Conference takes its origin from the fact that the Church draws its life's blood from the rural areas. Big cities do not reproduce themselves. If any big city of 100,000 or more population were walled off and no new citizens allowed to immigrate from outside, that city would die off at the rate of about twenty per cent in every generation. The story in the rural communities is quite the contrary; there the birthrate provides an increase of about twenty-five per cent in each generation—and it is this surplus, moving to the cities, which keeps the cities going.

In view of the fact that the Catholic Church in America is so largely an *urban* Church, there is no exaggerating the importance of having a strong Catholic element included in the influx from the country. As the country feeds the city, so will the country Church feed the city

Church. The National Catholic Rural Life Conference consequently has a three-fold aim: To keep on the land the Catholic families which already are there by making life on the land more attractive, economically and socially as well as religiously; then to attract more Catholics to rural areas, especially through the rural homestead idea— "one foot on the land and one foot in the city"—working in a town but living in the country; and finally to win to the Faith more of the non-Catholics who already are on farms and in rural communities.

It is a farsighted and genuinely missionary work. To make a thorough study of rural sociology, to attend the study weeks and conferences for the clergy which the NCRLC sponsors, to attend and participate in the annual conventions of the NCRLC—in short, to become an active expert in this whole field; what better hobby, if we may call it that, could a priest ask for? Besides the good one can accomplish, a priest who becomes actively interested in a movement such as this meets and makes friends with priests from other parts of the nation. His own vision is necessarily broadened as he hears of the problems that are being faced and the efforts that are being made in other sections of the country. In addition to the fellowship of a common priesthood, he establishes with priests from everywhere, close personal ties rooted in a common interest and zeal. There are many rewards to a hobby of this kind.

Of similar value is the Liturgical Movement, centered in America in a loosely knit organization known as The Liturgical Conference. The purpose of the Liturgical Conference is to save Catholic life from the weakening effects of mere formalism, mere ritualism; to make Christ, Christ living in His Mass and His sacraments, the center of Christian worship and practice; to make the liturgy popular in the best sense of the word—so that the liturgy may be known, understood, loved, and participated in by all the people.

It is a big order, and up to now there are comparatively few who labor at the task. What more absorbing "hobby" could a priest develop than to become an expert in the liturgy; not just an expert in ceremonial and rubrics, which are only the letter and not the spirit of worship, but an expert in the liturgy seen as Christ living in His Church? He would attend the annual meeting of the Liturgical Conference, would this priest—the annual Liturgical Week held in a different diocese each year. He perhaps would attend the liturgical sections of such conventions as the Catholic Educational Association and the Confraternity of Christian Doctrine. He would drink deeply of the liturgical literature which is becoming increasingly plentiful (starting perhaps with Father Clifford Howell's *Of Sacraments and Sacrifice*); by word, by work and by pen he would promote the Liturgical Revival, not only in his own parish but in an ever-widening circle of influence.

These are but two specimens that I offer. There are other movements, any number, to which a priest might well channel whatever leisure time he may have, with profit both to himself and to God. There is, for further example, the field of specialized Catholic Action in which, up to now, the principal bottleneck seems to have been lack of clerical interest which stems from lack of clerical understanding, and a consequent lack of the expert spiritual direction which such movements as the Young Christian Workers and the Christian Family Movement so fundamentally need.

Then there is the area of social justice, as exemplified by such groups as the Catholic Interracial Councils, the Catholic labor organizations and guilds, the Co-operative movement, and others. All of them are designed to contribute, each in its own degree, to the total Christianization of society. And if all the priests in our whole country who are actively interested and involved in these groups and movements were gathered together in one place, I think that a fairly large church would hold them all. And wouldn't any of these intellectual and apostolic activities outrank by far the distinction of being the best golfer or bridge-player, the best TV expert or flower-gardener in our bailiwick? Not to mention the dubious distinction of being the most widely read in popular magazines or the outstanding social luminary of the community?

In suggesting movements and organizations that could well be the terminus for a clerical hobby, I have not of course touched upon those which are normally a part of every diocesan set-up, such as the National Council of Catholic Men, the National Council of Catholic Women and the National Council of Catholic Youth, the Holy Name Society, the sodalities and confraternities. These are tied in with and are a part of our work as parish priests. As such they will without question have our whole-hearted and enthusiastic support and co-operation.

There is one movement that has not, so far as I know, even been started yet, and which happily could be instigated by some priest as his "hobby." I refer to what might be called a Priests' Retreat Promotion League. Its members would promote Days of Recollection for the diocesan clergy. But more specifically each active member would be pledged to prepare a set of conferences for such a Day of Recollection, and would be ready to conduct such a Day when called upon (no doubt in some other diocese than his own!). Members of the League would be exhorted and encouraged to prepare a set of conferences for an entire priests' retreat. Someone has said that every man has in him the making of one good book. I think that every priest has within him the material for at least one good set of retreat conferences, if he has given any thought at all to his own priestly life and experience. If such a League were successfully functioning, the day might even come when diocesan priests' retreats would be conducted, as a general rule, by diocesan priests.

That is said with no disparagement at all to the Fathers of the religious Orders who have labored through the years to help us become better priests. I have reason to be grateful to many of them, and so have you. Our fundamental religious needs are pretty much the same, whether our allegiance is to a bishop or to a religious superior; ultimately the allegiance of all of us is to Christ.

But there is no gainsaying the fact that there are problems that we do *not* have in common, problems that are specifically those of the diocesan clergy, problems which no one can evaluate as well as one of ourselves. When the Jesuits have a retreat, a Jesuit conducts it, and rightly so. When the Benedictines have a retreat, a Benedictine conducts it, and rightly so. For their own Holy Rule, their particular problems and religious spirit, they need one of their own to interpret. So, I think, do we.

Why not then write, to begin with, just one conference on some phase of a parish priest's spiritual life or work and send it in to one of the priests' magazines or reviews? You may be surprised to find how eagerly they accept it and how easily they publish it. With that encouragement you will go on to write further conferences, whether for publication or for personal presentation; not for glory and even less for dollars. But simply that you may share the fruit of your meditation with others, as you wish they would share their hard-won victories (or defeats) with you. Here is a hobby that is a challenge to any priest. Bowling or wood-working or parlor-magic cannot hold a candle to it.

Some may be objecting: "Where is the time for such things? Isn't my first duty to my people? Have I got the right to be getting myself involved in these outside matters?" Well, if that objection comes from a priest who really and truly is completely immersed in thoroughly priestly work, with a bare minimum of time for bodily rest and mental relaxation, then I say the objection is wholly justified. Our first duty *is* to our present job. But it is my contention (a mild contention, and a diffident one) that with most of us more time than we suspect leaks from our day, like water from a dripping faucet; more time than we suspect, until we have begun to put that time to a constructive use and discover how much of it we can salvage.

Over and over again we need to remind ourselves, "My time is God's, all God's. None of it belongs to me for my sole use and self-satisfaction. Even my recreation must fit into God's scheme of things, must have a supernatural motive. What matter if I burn myself out, so that like a candle I burn myself out for God?" To spend and to be spent; that must be the sole ambition of the priest who would also be, as God wants all of us to be, a saint.

THE PERSPIRING PRIEST

If we undertake to analyze our priestly work, we find that our principal pastoral duties (aside from our Mass, which is our *supreme* priestly function, and aside from the administration of the sacraments) will fall under one of seven general headings. I would list them as follows: (1) preaching; (2) recruitment and instruction of converts; (3) care of the sick; (4) home visitation; (5) catechizing; (6) administration; and (7) social service.

Preaching is placed at the head of the list because, although we seem sometimes to forget it, the fact is that preaching is the most compulsory of all our pastoral obligations. It is the one thing which Jesus Christ repeatedly and emphatically commanded His apostles to do. The apostles took this duty so seriously that they ordained deacons for such tasks as baptizing and caring for the poor, in order to leave themselves more time for the publication of the Good Tidings. We, Christ's present-day apostles, dare not take more lightly than they this primary function of our pastoral office.

The presumption is that we *do* take it more lightly, if we may judge by the low repute into which preaching has fallen in our time. Bishop Fulton Sheen is a marvelous preacher. But, without belittling at all his undoubted natural genius, I think that Bishop Sheen's success is due mainly to the fact that he takes his duty of preaching *with dead seriousness*. He overlooks nothing that will contribute to the effective presentation of God's Word. He makes sure that he has something worth saying to begin with—and then he calls upon every physical resource—voice, gesture, and expression—to speak the truths of salvation in the most persuasive manner possible.

It was Thomas Edison who said that genius is one per cent inspiration and ninety-nine per cent perspiration. Bishop Sheen himself probably would be the first to agree that there are hundreds of priests in America with a voice as expressive as his own. Just as probably he would be reluctant to add that very few priests have his own profound sense of responsibility to their primary apostolic duty; very few priests are willing to put in the long hours of study and labor that have gone into the making of a Fulton Sheen. He is a giant by any standard, is Bishop Sheen. But he looms the larger because most of the rest of us have chosen to remain so much smaller than we need to be.

Your own experience will bear me out that it is not an uncommon thing on Saturday night, after the post-confessional snack from the refrigerator, to hear a conversation something like this: Father A yawns and stretches and says, "Well, I'd better get to my room and think up a few words to say for tomorrow morning." "Don't be in a hurry," answers Father B; "it's an easy Gospel, the one about the paralytic; you can preach on Confession." And so, for the umpteenth time in as many years, the people will hear a stereotyped talk on Confession. Maybe not a very lucid or connected talk, either.

There will be a church full of people in need of bread, and they will be offered cracker crumbs.

It is not my intention to discuss at length our duty of preaching, except to emphasize again that it is our foremost pastoral obligation, one certainly upon which God will very strictly judge us. If every priest in America began to spend one hour a day, five days a week, on the preparation of his Sunday sermon, can we even estimate the revolution it might effect in the lives of our people? The Gospel of Christ is perennially new. It has application to the problems of *today*; the problems of the working man, the problems of the family, the problems of youth—all trying to live a Christian life in a secular world. But it takes work to dig those applications out and present them in a way that will make them vivid and practical to our hearers. So often we complain that our people are worldly, our families materialistic, our parents irresponsible and our youth semi-delinquent. What a horrible condemnation that is of ourselves! Because whose is the ultimate fault if not ours, since ours is the duty to inculcate the spirit of Christ? And where shall the reformation begin, if it does not begin in the pulpit?

We listed the recruitment and instruction of converts as the second type of pastoral work to which our time is given. Our self-examination on this point probably will not be too humbling, at least so far as the actual giving of instructions is concerned. We do welcome every inquirer. Our greatest danger here, particularly if we ourselves are unimaginative, is that we may fail to understand what a tremendous effort sometimes lies behind that first ringing of our doorbell; what a world-shaking event it is to the prospective convert when he first faces us in our office. Because it is such an old story to us, we are likely to manifest a casualness that may seem like coldness and indifference to this man or woman who is meeting a priest for the first time.

Have you ever had this experience: have you ever gone into a store to buy something, and been waited on by a clerk who seemed apathetic and uninterested, bored by having to serve you; who seemed to think he was doing you a favor by taking your money? I know that it has happened to me, and I never have felt any urge to go back to that store again. When a prospective convert comes to us, maybe we *are* doing him a favor by opening to him the door of the fold of Christ; but *he* doesn't know that yet. Even if we are suffering from a nagging headache or a touch of indigestion, we still need to show a warm and personal interest in the inquirer, to take seriously what is a very serious matter to him, to show a cordiality that will still his trepidation and convince him from the start that it is a *friendly* Christ Whom he will find in the Catholic Church. It is a warm and friendly interest that will continue through the term of his instructions; it will encourage him to talk a little about himself and his problems; it will be as patient with his questions as though we had not heard them all a thousand times before; it will keep us to an unhurried pace that will match his slowness. And of course our sense of responsibility to the catechumen will make us almost break our necks to keep our appointments with him—no matter what enticing invitations we may have to refuse, no matter what enjoyable visits we may have to cut short. He must never be let feel that he is a matter of minor importance to us, because factually he is a matter of major importance to Christ the Good Shepherd. We shall never fail in our duty to our converts if we keep always in mind that first impressions are the most lasting. For the rest of his life the Catholic Church will mean to this man pretty much what you or I, the instructor, have meant to him.

There is one other point in connection with our convert work that will bear repeating. Sometimes we are very conscientious in the duty of instructing, but very lax in the duty of recruiting. The fact that we have an established hierarchy in our country removes us technically from the ranks of missionary countries—but it does not remove us in fact. We do live in a missionary country, so long as there are unchurched millions around us. An inquiry class seems almost a must, at least in the larger parishes, if we are to go after the lost sheep in a serious way. But whether in inquiry classes or in private instructions, our zeal will leave no tool unused—mail campaign, house-to-house canvass, personal invitation through ourselves and our parishioners—no tool unused to enlist the interest of those who, often without knowing it, are seeking Christ. Through us, Christ will go in search for them.

The third on our list of parochial responsibilities is the care of the sick. I do not mean the administration of the Last Sacraments; we surely have no need to examine ourselves on that. I am referring rather to that care of the sick which goes beyond the bare essentials, that compassion for sufferers which is so constantly manifested by Christ throughout the Gospels. It is so *easy* to forget the sick, particularly in a large parish. We are called to a sick-bed; we go; we do what is necessary; then we become immersed in other duties and do not think of the sick person perhaps until we are called again.

Yet, after preaching and convert work, it would seem

G

that attention to the sick should be the most urgent of our pastoral activities. There are few things that we do in our parish which will bring upon us greater blessings from our Master than the time we give to those who are sharing in His Passion. The actual time involved is not so great, either. Even in a fairly large parish, one afternoon should be enough to make the rounds of the sick, to pay a short and cheerful call, to speak a word of encouraging reminder that will enable them to spiritualize their sufferings, to leave with them our priestly blessing. Those of us who have been priests many years, and who in time of sickness have any number of priest visitors can too easily forget what a visit from the pastor can mean to the ill of the parish.

We should be zealous too in bringing them Holy Communion, in breaking for them the Bread of Life when they need It the most. Once a week will not be considered too often by a selfless priest; and the selfless priest will not wait for the invalid to make the request, as he may be reluctant to do. The pastor himself will urge frequent Holy Communion, even though it may mean going out two or three mornings a week on such calls. Honestly, can we think of any better way, any more Christ-like way of spending our time? We may be tempted to say, "Why, that fellow doesn't go to Communion once a month when he's well! Why should I kill myself taking him Holy Communion every week, now that he's sick?" We cannot imagine any such words on the lips of Christ; they should not be on ours. Indeed, now is the time to teach the poor fellow the importance of Holy Communion. He will not be wholly unmindful of the sacrifices we are making to come to him; he may remember that if and when he gets well.

Just one other little thought with regard to the sick: if we have their phone numbers listed, it is a magnanimous thing to take maybe five minutes just before or after supper, and perhaps twice a week phone their homes to inquire as to the sick persons' progress, and to ask to be remembered to them. Such spontaneous attention on the part of a priest will never be forgotten. What a comfort it will be to us when we lie on our own sick-bed, to know that in times past we did everything within our power to make more bearable the sufferings of others.

So much for the sick, the aged and the ailing. Now what about our healthy parishioners? Our deepest and most lasting impression upon them, as I think every priest realizes, will be through the visits we make to their homes. When we reach into the home, we reach into the heart of every parishioner: the adult, the adolescent and the child. Once the priest has been in the home, every member of the family feels that a personal bond has been established with the priest, a bond whose intimacy nothing else can equal. The priest has been in their home. He knows what their house looks like, what pictures hang on the wall; he has seen the old sofa with the saggy cushions. He knows something of their problems—and the blessing he has left behind will make the problems seem a little lighter. From that visit on, every member of the family will feel a little closer to the priest, a little more receptive to his words from the pulpit and his words in the confessional.

This will be true even though all members of the family were not at home at the time of the priest's call. More likely than not, they will not all be at home. By force of circumstances, most home visitation must be done in the afternoon; some of the children may be in school, Dad may be at work. But it is enough for them to hear, when they get home, that the priest has been there; to listen, as Mother relates what she said to Father and what Father said to her.

It is probably the toughest work in the parish, this home visitation. In and out of the car, climbing steps, ringing doorbells, meeting strangers, going through the same conversations while preserving our cheerfulness and interest and putting others at their ease with us. It is just about the most tiring work there is, which perhaps is why we so often occupy ourselves with other things so that we can quiet our conscience with the plea that we are too busy. It is the hardest work we do, but it is the most rewarding, too. The soundest parishes in any diocese, materially as well as spiritually, will be those where the priests, like true Good Shepherds, are knocking at the doors. Do we plead lack of time? Well, I shall not say it, but Christ would say it: "We must make time!"

Catechizing is next on our list of labors. Ours is the responsibility to see that our children are instructed in Christian truth and their characters formed on a Christian pattern. Ours is a secondary responsibility, since parental obligation is primary here. But ours is the onus of reinforcing the work of the parents who do take their accountability seriously, and of substituting for those parents who take their liability lightly. Unlike preaching, convert instruction, sick care and home visitation, this is a duty which we can to a great extent discharge through delegates. In fact it is a duty which we must discharge through delegates, if there is to be time for the things that only the priest can do. If we have a parochial school, then the Sisters will be our delegates, both in the school and for the public school children after school hours. As helpers to the Sisters, and in place of the Sisters when the latter are lacking, will be our lay teachers, trained through our parish Confraternity of Christian Doctrine.

The priest of course will not be an unknown figure in the classroom and in the Confraternity classes. But I think that it is a great mistake for a priest to spend all morning every morning teaching in school, if more essential work must thereby be neglected. A single visit to a home sometimes can be worth a week spent in the school, so long as there are other qualified persons to teach the catechism. Of course, if the time taken from school is frittered away on *less* essential things—then conscience indeed would be in need of stirring up.

Another place from which we can pick up some of the time needed for more exigent obligations is from our sixth field of pastoral duty. I am ashamed to say that I know that from my own experience. Administration—which means making repairs, buying supplies, paying the bills, instituting new construction when needed—can be very interesting; much more fascinating than grinding away at a sermon, punching doorbells, or inhaling sickroom odors. The Old Man that is in us all will sometimes seek to complicate and magnify administrative tasks beyond all necessity, until there is no time for anything else on our agenda.

Here is where a searching honesty may uncover nuggets of time that a sly self-love has been carefully hiding. For example, can't I trust a competent architect and an experienced contractor to do a good job on the new building, instead of spending most of every day stumbling over bricks and beams myself? Can't I let the sexton order his own janitor supplies? Can't I let the sacristan order

candles and Mass wine as needed? Can't the housekeeper
look after her own minor replacements and repairs about
the house, calling in plumber or electrician herself as any
capable housewife would? Isn't there an accountant in
the parish who for a few dollars would come in one
evening a week to keep the parish books?

If we find ourselves pressed for time for the perform-
ance of genuinely priestly work, then we should ask
ourselves, when faced with any other task, "Is this something that a layman could do?" If it is, then why not
let a layman do it? I can look back, myself, and recall
occasions when I would spend a whole day running
around town on errands that anyone could have taken
care of, or that ten minutes on the phone might have
done as well; unconsciously killing time that could have
been given to some less welcome but more pastoral task.
If we find ourselves unduly bogged down in administration, we probably tell ourselves that we are doing it to
save the parish money. "This is the money of the poor,"
we say, "I can't be careless with it." No, we cannot be
careless with it. But the souls of the poor are even more
important than their money. If I save a dollar, or ten,
while a soul is being lost, where is the *quid pro quo?*

That brings us, finally, to the seventh area of parochial
functioning—the one that I have listed, for want of a
better term, under the heading of "social service." Within
this rather elastic division we might group such matters
(I hardly can say "duties") as the sponsoring of athletic
teams, the organization of recreational activities, the promotion of parish social affairs and fund-raising activities.
Just as the realm of administration is by necessity the job
of the pastor, so the realm of "social service" is usually,
by common agreement, the job of the assistant where

there is one. When it comes to salvaging the time that is needed for essential pastoral duties, there is more gold in this last field than can be reclaimed even from administrative work. It seems tragic that a young man whose priesthood represents twenty years of schooling, the investment of thousands of dollars in money, and uncounted sacrifices on the part of so many people; a young man who possesses miraculous powers that are given to few—it seems tragic that he should end up on a playfield coaching the eighth-grade ball team, or in the gym managing the high school basketball team, or combing the town for prizes for the annual fiesta.

He likes these things, sure. They are much more fun than writing a sermon with fire and life in it, than scouting out converts, than fortifying the sick and visiting homes. But we were not ordained to do the things we like, in a natural sense. We were ordained to do the things that God likes, however burdensome to ourselves. I did all these things when I was an assistant. Looking back now, I am certain that, under God, I would have done far more good for souls if the hours I spent on playfield, in gymnasium, and in parish hall had been spent instead in sermon preparation and home visitation. This whole field is one in which competent laymen can do as good a job—in many cases a better job—than a priest. If it costs money to hire a coach or an athletic director—well, what price shall we put on a priest? And if the parish cannot afford to hire a layman, and there are no volunteers, then the game is just not worth the candle. We need to have contact with our young people, sure. But the normal contacts we shall have with them as we go cheerfully about our work in the parish will do them more spiritual good in the end than long hours spent with a selected few who see us only as a man rather than as a priest.

There are other things that fill our days besides the seven major spheres that I have mentioned. There is the personal counselling of individuals who come to us for advice. There are the marriage cases to be worked on, there is spiritual direction to be given to our parish societies, there are letters to answer, and there are a lot of other things. It was not for nothing that I headed this piece, "The Perspiring Priest." But, before any of us plead a lack of time for the priestly duties that only we can do, I beg that we may analyze our day with merciless realism; and as we go over it item by item, let us ask ourselves, "How much of this can be done by a layman; indeed, how much of it could be left undone with no real harm to souls?"

THE MARIAN PRIEST

MANY OF US have the Sodality of Our Lady established in our parishes and consequently discharge the office of spiritual director to our Sodality group. I wonder how many of us have ever noticed what a wonderful *précis* of a priest's relationship to Mary is contained in Sodality rule number forty? Let me quote the rule here, substituting the word "priest" for the word "Sodalist": "The Blessed Virgin Mary is the principal patroness of the priest. Hence priests should make profession of a particular devotion to her and strive to imitate her splendid virtues, place all confidence in her, and urge one another on to love and serve her with filial devotedness." Can anyone improve upon that as an outline of a priest's duty to the Mother of God?

A patron, we know, is someone who backs another up in something that other person is trying to do. If a group of boys want to start a baseball team but have no money for uniforms or equipment, they look around for a patron. Perhaps some goodhearted man, maybe a local merchant will say, "Sure boys, I'll pay for your uniforms and supplies. Anything you need, you come to me; I'll stand behind you." That man will be the patron of the team.

G*

Or maybe there is a promising boy in our parish who wants to go to the seminary, but his parents are poor and cannot afford the tuition and books during the preparatory years. We call the youngster in and say, "Look, Jimmie: you go along to the seminary; I'm going to tell the rector to send all your bills to me. I'll see that you get a little spending money from time to time, too. And if you ever need any money for clothes and such, you just let me know. I'll be behind you one hundred per cent." We, manifestly, would be the lad's patron.

In both cases we see that a patron is someone who lends solid support in enabling us to accomplish something we want to do. So, when we speak of Our Blessed Mother as our Patroness, we mean that she is the one whom we can look to, to sustain us in all our needs, to back us up in the biggest job of our lives, the thing we want most to do: the business of becoming a saint. If Mary is tremendously interested in every soul for whom Christ died, there just is no overestimating her interest in us who are so close to and so dear to her Son, who are such necessary channels through which the fruits of her Son's Passion must flow to others.

And she has so much to give. She is the one to whom Our Lord has entrusted the distribution of His graces. Because of His love for her, Jesus lets flow through Mary's hands the graces which He gained for us by His death upon the cross. Just as Jesus came to us through Mary in the first place, so now He gives us His graces through her hands. That is why the Church calls Mary "The Mediatrix of all grace." If we imagine Jesus as seated on His throne in Heaven, then we think of Mary as seated upon a throne next to Him—the Queen Mother next to the King. When we come to the King with outstretched hands, He turns to the Queen and says, "Mother, shall we give this child what he asks?" And Mary smiles and reaches into the royal treasure-chest and hands us the gift. If that sounds too whimsical, too coy, I just do not know how else we can express in human imagery the great and beautiful truth of Mary's intercessory power.

She is our Patroness. God knows—no one better—what need we have of her help and her support. We need her backing in our own weaknesses and imperfections, in removing some of our own shabbiness as Christians and as priests. We need her sustenance too in our labor for souls, in our often disheartening labors with the lax, the hard-of-heart, the fallen-aways. Here, since our own sanctification necessarily works itself out so largely through our efforts towards the sanctification of others, there is a double dividend for ourselves when Mary's patronage applies the leverage that our own words and pains could not produce. Pitiable indeed would be the priest who would feel so secure in his own loftiness as to feel no need for Mary; perhaps even reversing the roles and according the Mother of God the patronizing deference of the strong towards the weak.

Mary is our Patroness, and towards her we should have a "filial devotedness." "Filial," of course, means childlike; it means the kind of feeling that a child has towards his mother. It conjures up a picture of a little fellow hanging on to Mother's skirts, not wanting to get very far away from Mother, running to Mother if he stubs his toe or scratches his hand or when danger threatens, feeling that Mother is the most wonderful person in all the world. That is the kind of feeling that we as priests should strive to have towards Mary our

Patroness. This "filial devotedness," if we have it, will show itself principally in four ways:

First of all by the "particular devotion" that we have to Mary. If we go back to the example of the boy whom we send to the seminary and whose education we finance, I think we can see that such a lad would pay us a lot of attention. He would write to us regularly; he would come to see us every time he got home for a holiday; he would show us his report card and joyfully tell us of his successes—and maybe seek our comfort in his failures; he probably would want to have us over to his house to dinner, and would gratefully bring us some little gift for Christmas and maybe for our birthday.

It is that same kind of devotion that we should nurture towards our Patroness, our Mother Mary. We should honor her because she is so deserving of honor—but especially we should honor her for what she is doing for us. No doubt all of us have a picture or a statue of Mary in our study and in our bedroom and often think of her as our eyes fall upon her image; maybe hurrying in or hurrying out, yet still finding time for a quick "Mary my Mother, pray for me!" Probably, too, many of us make her Litany a regular part of our morning prayers or night prayers, or one of our prayers during our daily visit to her Son in the tabernacle. No doubt we welcome those Saturdays on which we can offer Mary's Mass; it does seem that we should hesitate to offer a Black Mass, unless it is really necessary, on a day when "*Maria in sabbato*" is permitted. But at least on Mary's feast days there will be a keen consciousness, a loving recollection, of her whom we are honoring.

One practice which I am certain that all of us have is the daily recitation of the Rosary. That is a practice that ought to be a habit with any good Catholic. It is a positive *must* (a moral, not a legal "must") for the priest. Well as we know it, it might be worth while for us to recall that we must *meditate* on the Mysteries of the Rosary in order to gain the indulgences; to recall the fact, and to ask ourselves how well we acquit ourselves of that requirement. The Rosary is somewhat in the nature of a duet. Just as piano and violin can unite in one beautiful piece of music—the piano playing the obbligato and the violin carrying the melody—so, too, in the Rosary the vocal organs play the accompaniment with their cadenced *Paters* and *Aves*, while the mind carries the solo part as it dwells lovingly on the Mysteries.

There is the first Joyful Mystery, for example: the Annunciation. We see the Archangel Gabriel as he appears to Mary to announce to her that she is to be the Mother of God. While our lips busy themselves with the Our Fathers and the Hail Marys, our mind is occupied with what is happening. We try to picture Mary as she really looked: a dark-eyed, dark-haired, beautiful girl of fifteen. Perhaps she is standing lost in prayer; perhaps she is pushing a broom as she helps St. Anne with the housework. Suddenly the room is filled with a brilliant light, and there is the angel standing in front of Mary. (I always have trouble trying to picture angels to myself; usually I think of them in the guise of a particularly youthful and handsome bishop.) In any case, Mary would be the last one in the world to expect a messenger from God to appear to her. It is no wonder that she is startled and confused. "Hail, full of grace!" the angel says; and Mary hardly knows what he is talking about. We know it now, but she didn't know it then—that her soul was so perfectly pure and holy that there wasn't room in it at that moment for even a slight addition of grace. She is too humble to think of herself as anything special. The Gospel says that "She was troubled at his word."

But Gabriel didn't give her much time to think. He went right on to tell her that she would conceive and bear a Son whose name would be called Jesus; and that her Child would be the son of the Most High. It is all so sudden, Mary hardly knows what to say; her mind is going around in circles. Since early childhood she has given herself completely to God; she has made the vow of virginity; she has dedicated her life entirely to the service of God; and now suddenly she is told that she is to be a mother. "How will this be?" Mary asks, "since I do not know man?" In other words, How can I be a mother without breaking my vow of chastity? Then the angel tells her that her child will not have a human father. "The Holy Ghost shall come upon thee," the angel says, "and the power of the Most High shall overshadow thee; and therefore the Holy One to be born shall be called the Son of God."

The moment that Mary understands that there will be no conflict in her duty to God—that she still will be a virgin even though she is a mother, she bows her head in her "*Fiat*": "Be it done unto me according to Thy word." All my plans are upset now, Mary may have thought to herself; I just wanted to live a quiet and simple life, away from the confusion and the turmoil of the world. Now I shall be surrounded by worries and sorrow and mixed up in so many things that I can only dimly see. It isn't what I had planned (Mary may have continued to herself), but if that is what God wants, then that is what I want too.

Then at this point of our meditation on the first Joyful

Mystery we turn our thoughts to ourselves, to make our meditation fruitful. How about me? Is what-God-wants more important to me than what-I-want? If things don't pan out the way I want them to, do I get angry and resentful, complain about the bad luck or the injustice, and wallow in self-pity? Am I as quick to accept God's will as Mary was, even when it seems to turn everything topsy-turvy for me? Well, I'll try to be more patient after this, more cheerful and calm when things go wrong.

That is only one of many possible meditations on the first Mystery of the Rosary. There are other lessons that we can find for ourselves; our thoughts will not be the same every day. One time we may think of how necessary it is for us to pray if we hope to hear God's voice in impulses of grace; just as Mary was praying when God sent His angel. Another time we may think of how necessary it is for us to be humble, to be little in our own eyes, if we are going to be useful instruments for God's own purposes. Yes, there will be many other lessons that we shall find for ourselves in the fifteen decades of the Rosary, as day after day we manifest this devotion to our Patroness.

Then, besides having a particular devotion to our Patroness, we shall "strive to imitate her splendid virtues." We shall imitate Mary in her simplicity, in her self-effacement, in her joyfulness in humble tasks, in the utter limpidity of her sincerity, in the singleness of her love, in the courage with which she followed the cross. We need a model to follow, in fashioning our lives as Christians and as priests. In the making of anything worthwhile, we do best when we follow a model. If our tailor tried to make us a suit without following a pattern, it would hang on us like a potato sack; we'd be tempted to throw it back in his face. If our housekeeper baked a cake without using a recipe, we'd find ourselves facing a messy goo or a pastry brick that would send us quickly from the table. If we started on a motor trip to a strange destination without a road-map to follow, we'd end up in the middle of nowhere. If a pastor undertook to build a church without a plan, a blueprint to follow, his parishioners would curse the resultant monstrosity.

Whatever we do, it is so much easier to accomplish it well if we have a model to follow, whether we call the model a pattern or a recipe or a road-map or a blueprint. This is true above all in building a truly priestly life, a truly Christ-like life for ourselves. Christ Himself is, of course, our model. If we try to pattern ourselves on Christ, if we try to live and think and talk and act as He would in our place—then we know that we shall be exemplary priests, saintly priests. That is one of the three things Christ came upon earth to do; to *show* us the way to sanctity. He not only came to teach us the truths we need to know; He not only came to open the gates of Heaven by His death on the Cross; He came also *to show us how to live.* "I am the Way," He says, "and the Truth and the Life." He puts "the Way" first of all.

But we may be tempted to say, "That's a big order! How can I ever hope to really imitate Jesus Christ? It's true that He is a human being, but He also is God, with all the sanctity of God. I never could hope to be holy as He is holy." Jesus Himself foresaw that difficulty. He realized that we might get discouraged at the thought of imitating Him. So He gave us someone who is *all* human, and yet is a perfect image of Christ; He gave us Mary, His own Mother, to be what we might call our secondary model. When we contemplate Mary, we are seeing what a human being is like when he or she perfectly reflects Christ. If we imitate Mary, we are imitating Christ. If we become Mary-like, we cannot help but become Christ-like. We do not have two models, Christ *and* Mary; we have but one model: Christ *through* Mary. If we follow her, we follow Him; and there is no surer guide.

Besides having a particular devotion to Mary, and striving to imitate her splendid example, the priest will "place all confidence in her." That means that in all times of trouble, trial, discouragement—whenever the going gets tough—Mary is the one we turn to first. It matters not whether the cross is a personal one: temptation, or sickness, or grief; or whether the cross is a pastoral one: an apostate parishioner, a school scandal, a financial crisis—we go to Mary with complete confidence; we know that she will not betray our trust, she will not let us down. No one except God Himself, just no one is as interested in us as Mary is. Our bishop, our priest friends, our own family—not one of them can be one-thousandth or one-hundred thousandth as interested in helping us make good as our Blessed Mother is. Remember that she stood at the foot of the cross and watched the blood flowing from wounds in the hands and feet and face of Jesus—to her, still her Little Boy. She counted the drops of blood as they fell one by one and made a red mud at her feet. She does not want to see a single drop of that blood wasted; she does not want her Son to lose a single soul for whom He died. This is true of every soul—but how much greater must be her zeal and compassion for those of us who bear the mark of Her Son's priesthood!

Finally, as protégés of Mary our Patroness, we should "urge one another on to love and serve her." In some dioceses priests have carried that out literally by organiz-

ing themselves into Priests' Sodalities. I think myself that
such Sodalities can be a great help towards fuller priestliness. But it is not so much in our contacts with each
other as it is in our leadership of the whole body of the
faithful that we can and should demonstrate our zeal for
the honor of Mary. It is a strange phenomenon, but really
it sometimes seems that our laity have a greater devotion
to Mary than we priests do. So often our approach to
Mary seems to remain on a formal—what we might call
an "official"—level. We seem to lack the intensity so
often, the *simplicity* of love and confidence, that the
average lay-person has. I fear that in this their instinct is
more trustworthy than our own. The very universality
of the common Catholic's urge towards Mary, the very
naturalness of his attraction to her, ought to make suspect
the coolness of our own sentiments, if cool they be.

How can we account for this strange gap which sometimes exists between the faith of the faithful and the
faith of the priest? Perhaps we would say that our own
devotion to Mary is more "realistic," less tinged with
superstition. But may it not be possible that it is we who
are tinged—not with superstition, but with intellectual
pride? May it not be that ours is the attitude of one who
knows too much because he does not know enough—the
attitude of one who has progressed too far to be simple,
and not far enough to become simple again? It is never
the saints who put a check-rein and a measure on their
devotion to Mary.

How often during the past year have we preached on
the Mother of God, aside from such times as the feast or
the occasion made it inescapably necessary? Does her
name, and at least passing reference to her, come frequently into our sermons? If there are souls in our

parish banded together under the aegis of Mary—a Sodality, the Legion of Mary, the Rosary Confraternity—do they have our active encouragement, are we zealous to see that they do not forget the glory of their Patroness? There is, of course, a limitation of time upon what a priest himself can do; but do we at least give our blessing and make it plain that we are behind them, if some of our parishioners wish to undertake some Marian activity such as the Scapular Militia or the Block Rosary?

It is all very well to talk of putting first things first. But who is to judge as to the relative importance of doctrines and devotions—we, or God? Surely it is not without reason that Our Lord again and again sends His Mother into the world with His messages. Our Lord knows that we shall never forget Him; it is rarely that He makes a public or a heralded appearance Himself; His apparition to St. Margaret Mary is the only instance that I can, offhand, remember. But again and again He sends His Mother to speak to us, it seems at least once in every generation. And He is bountiful with His wonders, whether it be water gushing from the earth or the sun dancing in the sky; and He is lavish with His miracles, of healing and of grace—to make sure that His Mother's coming does not go unnoticed and unremarked. Christ has made His own mind plain enough; His mind surely must be the mind of His priests.

And if I have sounded a bit as though I were scolding, it is not so. You see, I have been talking, really, to myself. "Mary, Queen of Apostles, pray for us—pray for us! Pray for this tepid heart!"

THE ARDENT PRIEST

RECENTLY in a magazine article written by a Catholic layman I ran across a descriptive definition of the priesthood which I have not since been able to get out of my mind. A priest, said this writer, is "a man who has risked almost everything in a Divine Game in which a glowing sanctity and a particular dry rot of the soul are the frightening alternatives."[1] You have to think of that for a minute to get the full truth of it, the full impact of it. Glowing sanctity or dry rot. Along either one of those two roads each of us is traveling. Not that we have yet arrived. None of us I am sure would claim to have achieved a glowing sanctity, and none of us I hope has reached the state of utter collapse which is the last sudden stage in dry rot. But we are heading in one direction or the other; there is no middle road.

We all know what dry rot is like. There is no odor of corruption about it. There is no softness to the touch. Usually there is no outward discoloration. There is just a steady, day-by-day deterioration and decay—all inward until the very end.

The priest who is on that road is the priest who has lost

---

[1] Erik von Kuehnelt-Leddihn in *Commonweal*.

his sense of the supernatural. I do not say a priest who has lost his faith; but a priest whose faith is no longer a living reality, no longer the vital principle of his priestly life and work. He is a priest whose approach to his work is a professional approach rather than an apostolic approach. He may be a hard-working priest, a respected priest, what we commonly term a successful priest. But his prime interest will be in the external phases of his work; size and numbers will mean more to him than the hidden workings of grace. The last-minute salvation of some poor derelict will leave him unimpressed, but a thousand people at a novena service will send him back to the rectory smiling. He will come into the quiet church to empty the votive boxes, and will leave again with barely the courtesy of a skimpy genuflection to the altar. He will escape hearing confessions if it is at all possible, since to him the hearing of confessions seems such unrewarding drudgery. If he cannot escape it, then the slides of his box will open and shut, open and shut, with nothing more than the mechanical dispensing of a conventional penance. He will celebrate his Mass punctually on working days, but on vacation his Mass will be just another part of the whole routine from which he gladly escapes.

His approach to his work, I have said, is the professional approach. He does the work of the priesthood very much as some men do the work of the world. It's a job to be done, the job he was trained for, the job he is paid for—even if the pay isn't very much. "It's one way of making a living," he even may say, wryly and only half joking. He manages to find a generous amount of time for his favorite pastimes and recreations. There is not much danger that he'll chuck things completely; it would create too much confusion in his life, and the future would be too uncertain. Besides, his faith hasn't actually died; it just lies dormant.

That would be, quite literally, a *hell* of a way for a priest to live, wouldn't it? To live one's life on a natural level, with no odor or ugliness of decay to give one warning? And it could happen to anyone. It could happen, it *will* happen, to any priest who has let himself lose touch with the core and center of his priestly life and work: Jesus in the Most Blessed Sacrament.

Think of what it means if we grow lax in our devotion to Christ in the tabernacle. *He* is the One we are working for—not for the Pope or the Bishop or our stipends and stole fees. What a loss to us in holy skill and joy and fruitfulness if we drift away from personal contact with Him. What a tragedy if He becomes just one of our many duties, just Something to be cared for and kept in plentiful supply and dispensed to our people!

To what other teacher can we go, except to Jesus in the Blessed Sacrament, to learn the lessons in priestly and pastoral virtue which we do have to learn every day, over and over again? Who better than He can teach us the lesson of humility, for example? He was not content to spend thirty years in the obscurity of Nazareth, with His divine power hidden and unused. He was not content to be for three years misunderstood and rejected, tied to twelve men whose faith was so little and who were so slow to understand the truths He tried to spell out for them; preaching of Heaven to people who only wanted an earthly kingdom, people who ate His bread and His fish and then forgot Him. He was not content to "empty Himself" on Calvary in obedience to His Father and for love of us, allowing His Humanity to taste the dregs of utter failure and defeat. He was not content with this: He chose to all but annihilate Himself completely in the Eucharist, hiding His face and stilling His voice that He might remain through all time with the souls for whom He died as their Sacrifice and their Food, shepherding them silently before Him towards the joy He has prepared for them. Probably it is thoroughly untheological, but I like to think that Jesus died upon the cross in obedience to His Father's Will; but that remaining with us in the Eucharist was His own idea; in the end He just couldn't bear the thought of leaving us to fend for ourselves.

Here then, before the tabernacle, is where we learn humility. Here is where the petty triumphs of which we like to talk (casually, of course, but always working them into the conversation) now seem silly and shabby. Here is where the complaints we have made of the burden of our work and the lack of appreciation we have encountered are regurgitated and taste like quinine on our lips. Here is where we drop the magnifying glass from before our eyes and see the true smallness of our bigness —see, as the angels see, the paucity of our sacrifices and the stinginess of our so-carefully-measured sweat.

Yes, in the presence of Jesus in the Blessed Sacrament we learn humility, if we will let Him teach us, and we learn zeal too. "My God what a day!" we say as we come into the church mopping our brow. And there before us is He Who escaped from the crowds to spend the night in prayer, and came down from the mountain to be swallowed up by the greedy crowds again. He was pushed and hauled and all but trampled upon—and He was human, remember, and felt fatigue as we do. If He sat for a moment to rest, there were the mothers pushing

their children at Him—and His arms open to receive
them. And what care He had for the sick—everywhere
He went He watched for them—at the Pool of Bethsaida
or on the Temple steps. They had first claim upon His
time; He would stop in the middle of a discourse to heal
the palsied man, He would let His dinner wait while He
healed Peter's mother-in-law. "My meat is to do the will
of Him that sent Me," Jesus says: *that* is the lesson He
will teach us, if we give Him the chance.

But of course there can be no true zeal unless first
there is love for souls. It is this love for souls, above all
else, that Jesus can little by little impart to us and increase
in us as we kneel before the tabernacle. Not love for
souls in the mass, love for souls in the abstract—but love
for this soul and that soul. Jesus does not love you nor
me as one little unit in the aggregate. He loves you and
he loves me as though each of us was the only soul to
be loved, the only soul He had to think about. That is
the way we must love. It is easy to love souls at a distance. It is easy at least to *think* that we love souls, so
long as they remain just a sea of faces before us in the
pews. What about this soul right here on the chair in
our office—this mixed-up and confused person who can't
even talk sense- or this nasty-mouthed little person who
is just trying to fight off his own fears and insecurity—
or this apparently smugly sinful soul whose handicaps
of rearing and environment we can't begin to guess—
or this stupid soul whose stupidity is a matter of the
physical brain, but whose spirit within is as perfectly
fashioned by God as yours or mine? What about such
souls as these when they are dropped, in one way or
another, into our lap—do we love *them?* Christ would.
Christ does. And He will teach us how to do it too, in

the quiet moments we spend before the tabernacle. Then we shall begin to understand what is meant by the *compassion* of Christ, and we shall begin to feel a similar compassion and to manifest it to all. Obduracy will move us not to anger but to tears. Ill-will will arouse in us not resentment but pity. Stupidity will evoke from us not sharpness but gentle patience. And rather than condemn the souls we cannot reach and cannot change, we shall feel a rightful guilt for the defect in ourselves which hinders the flow of grace through us to them.

Which brings us to another fruit which we harvest from our devotion to Jesus in the Blessed Sacrament: the grace that will make up for our own deficiencies. The priest who lives his life on a supernatural level knows that no amount of scurry and clamor and breathlessness will mean a thing in the final balancing unless the energy is directed *to God* and is fused with and fortified by God's grace. He knows what it is to reason with a recalcitrant soul time after time without effect and to the point of discouragement—and then, after a humble plea before the tabernacle, have the person walk into the rectory and say, "Father, I've thought it all over, and you're right." He knows too, the priest who works for God, what it is to plan and work and worry at a project with nothing but apparent failure in the end—and then (a little late perhaps), after putting the whole thing before Jesus in the Blessed Sacrament, finding all the pieces miraculously falling into place. He knows likewise, the Eucharistic priest, the sure cure for a crowded schedule. When there are so many things to be done that he can't possibly do them all, he goes into church and spends maybe half an hour before the tabernacle. He finds that the half-hour he has given to Jesus seems to double all the rest of his time, while it cuts the burden of his duties in half.

That, if I may digress a moment, is something that many of us doubtless have discovered with regard to all our spiritual duties: time given to God comes back to us two and three times over. Show me the man who is faithful to his spiritual duties: to his Mass devoutly offered with preparation and thanksgiving, to his daily meditation, to the recollected recitation of his Office, to his daily Rosary and examen and visit to the Blessed Sacrament; and I will show you a man who gets more done in the course of a day, with less wear and tear, than the man who has time for nothing but a hasty Mass and a distracted Office, and rushes pell-mell through the rest of the day. That is the best answer, that is the only answer, to the priest who says that he is too busy to pray. And it is an answer that can very easily be tested by anyone who doubts it.

But to go back to results that flow from our particular devotion to Jesus in the Blessed Sacrament: Besides the graces we gain for our people (and they are *so* dependent upon us, their shepherds, for so much of their grace!) there are the graces we need and the graces we get for ourselves. There are the inspirations we need to do our best work for God. It is so easy to pass by, without even seeing, opportunities for accomplishing great good; opportunities that are only awaiting the touch of our hand. Somehow or another it so often seems to be during our visits to Jesus in the Blessed Sacrament that our eyes are unveiled to these opportunities; sometimes they seem so obvious then that we exclaim, "Now why didn't I think of that before?"

It is before the tabernacle too that we shall find the counsel and the guidance we need if there is to be confidence and sureness of touch in our undertakings. You must have felt at times, as I have, the poverty of the priest when it comes to guidance in his problems. Time and again we find ourselves faced with a decision to make. It may be a personal decision, it may be a parochial decision. There are good reasons on both sides, and there are doubtful points on both sides. We can't always be running to the bishop, and we shouldn't be. We have a confessor, a good and pious and helpful guide, but this isn't exactly a matter of sin or virtue; and it would be so hard to explain all the circumstances to him, anyway. That is true likewise of our priest friends; it is hard to make them see the problem as we would see it. Besides, they have problems of their own, and in spite of their friendship they are apt to give us a snap judgment on ours. We cannot hesitate and vacillate forever. Where is our recourse then?

The Eucharistic priest knows where his recourse is, when all human wisdom fails. He knows that quite literally he has a pipe-line to heaven—and its outlet is right there before him in the middle of the altar. He has only to go over his problem once, and listen prayerfully, contemplatively, for the answer—and he has it; with a certainty that no other counsellor could give.

It is here finally that we shall find healing for our wounds and comfort for our failures and courage for our crosses. It is here that we sometimes come like a bleeding dog dragging himself to the feet of his master. We thought that we did want to be good; we thought that we really were trying. And then a moment's forget-

fulness of our weakness can make such fools of us all.
And even as we bury our face in our hands and cry
silently, "O Jesus, I am so faithless, so ungrateful, so
undeserving of Your love!"—even as we say it there is
balm and there is strength in the grace that flows to us
from the tabernacle; and we raise our eyes to look upon
the invisible but pitying Christ with the renewed determination that we yet will be the man of God we want
to be. Perhaps we shall never be any stronger, but we
shall be wiser by His grace, more acute in seeing danger,
swifter to fling ourselves into His protecting embrace.

Yes, Fathers, we do need, we do *so* need, to have a
passionate devotion to Jesus in the Blessed Sacrament.
We do so need to build our lives around Him Who is
the whole reason for our being as priests. We do need to
come into His presence for that daily visit without which
a priest's life is an anomaly and a contradiction. Sometimes when we preach a sermon on the Blessed Sacrament
we chide our people because so few of them pay visits
during the week to the church. Well, it will not be by
our words that we propagate devotion in our parish to
Jesus in the Blessed Sacrament; at least not by our words
alone, not by our words most of all. Our own visits will
not be made primarily for purposes of edification. It may
well be that none of our people will ever see us as we
kneel before the Master's Throne. But surely we must
realize that we shall kindle a little blaze there whose flame
will spread without any conscious fanning of our own.

How long should our visit be? Only our own generosity can answer that. Only the firmness of our faith
in the fact that not a minute spent there will be wasted
can fix the length of our visit. It should be long enough

for the reality of Christ's Presence there to sink in, long enough for us to establish a sense of close personal communion with Him, as real to us as He was real to Peter and John as they might sit quietly talking together in the darkness on Galilee's shore. He *is* as real as that; and we must not only believe it, but we must experience the conviction of it. In the beginning it may take a little while for that conviction to grow upon us. The distractions of the world will drop from us slowly, and the vision that recollection gives will be the light of a slow dawning.

But as daily visit follows upon daily visit, our consciousness of Christ's Presence will come more quickly; our communication with Him will be more easily established. And who knows? The day may even come when we no longer make our visit from motives of holy selfishness: for the humility and zeal and compassion and love for souls that Jesus can teach us; for the graces we need for our people and for ourselves; for the inspirations and the comfort that Christ will give. Our love for our Hidden Master may grow to the point where we come solely because we know He wants us, because our own presence for some mysterious reason is pleasing to Him, because we respond to the pull of Him the way the earth responds to the pull of the sun.

Yes, the day even may come when we no longer ungraciously count the minutes we spend with Him, when we no longer ask ourselves, "Is this long enough?"; the day when we find ourselves reluctant to leave, forced almost to tear ourselves away, walking from the church with dragging feet, like a child sent early to bed. That day, I must confess, has not yet come for me. But it will not come for any of us unless day by day we give Jesus the chance to open our eyes and our hearts wider. Above all, it will never come unless we at least begin.

"Jesus in the Most Blessed Sacrament of the altar, help us your priests to love Thee, that we may live for Thee and Thee alone!"